You Should Read This Book If:

- You are not Jewish and you are married to or are dating someone who is.
- Your son, daughter, or anyone close to you who is not Jewish is dating or married to someone who is Jewish.
- You are a Jewish community leader, rabbi, cantor, or other professional serving the Jewish community seeking additional insights into interfaith marriages.
- You have friends in interfaith relationships and want to introduce them to the beauty of Judaism and the resources of the Jewish community.
- You are Jewish and looking for a framework through which to discuss Judaism with your non-Jewish spouse or partner.
- You are Jewish and seeking a resource for greater clarity about your own faith to better explain it to your non-Jewish spouse or someone you are dating.

While this book assumes that the reader comes from a Christian background (because the vast majority of Jewish interfaith relationships in North America are with Christians), this book is for everyone involved in Jewish interfaith relationships. If you are of a faith other than Christianity, you can still find meaning in these pages.

Some readers may consult this book on a quest for easy answers to the challenges they face in their interfaith relationships or as a practical "how-to" for Jewish living. However, rather than always giving the answers, in good Jewish tradition I offer you material to grapple with so that you can derive your own meaning and draw your own conclusions. Those seeking additional information or a step-by-step "how to" guide may want to refer to *The Rituals and Practices of a Jewish Life: A Handbook for Personal Spiritual Renewal* (Jewish Lights Publishing), which I coauthored with Rabbi Daniel Judson. For practical guidance in navigating an interfaith relationship, you may find helpful *Making a Successful Jewish Interfaith Marriage: The Jewish Outreach Institute Guide to Opportunities, Challenges and Resources* (Jewish Lights Publishing), which I coauthored with Joan Peterson Littman.

Introducing My Faith and My Community

The Jewish
Outreach
Institute
Guide for the
Christian in a
Jewish Interfaith
Relationship

RABBI KERRY M. OLITZKY

For People of All Faiths, All Backgrounds
JEWISH LIGHTS Publishing
Woodstock, Vermont

Introducing My Faith and My Community:
The Jewish Outreach Institute Guide for the Christian
in a Jewish Interfaith Relationship

First Printing 2004
© 2004 by Kerry M. Olitzky

Library of Congress Cataloging-in-Publication Data
Olitzky, Kerry M.
Introducing my faith and my community : the Jewish Outreach Institute guide for the Christian in a Jewish interfaith relationship / Kerry M. Olitzky.
p. cm.
Includes bibliographical references.
ISBN 1-58023-192-6 (pbk.)
1. Judaism. 2. Judaism—Relations. I. Jewish Outreach Institute. II. Title.
BM565.O45 2004
296'.02'423—dc22   2004004201

10 9 8 7 6 5 4 3 2 1

Manufactured in the United States of America
Cover design by Bridgett Taylor
Illustrations by Sara Dismukes

For People of All Faiths, All Backgrounds
Published by Jewish Lights Publishing
A Division of LongHill Partners, Inc.
Sunset Farm Offices, Route 4, P.O. Box 237
Woodstock, VT 05091
Tel: (802) 457-4000   Fax: (802) 457-4004
www.jewishlights.com

For Sarah Littman and Andréa Hanssen,
two special women who have enriched the life of our family
with their gifts of love and understanding.

Contents

Acknowledgments

Like the origins of so many of the books published by Jewish Lights Publishing, the idea for this particular book came as an invitation from my good friends and colleagues at Jewish Lights, Stuart and Antoinette Matlins. They are sensitive to the variety of needs in the Jewish community, and they also understand the challenges that partners encounter in an interfaith relationship. As I have told them so many times: my profound gratitude to you for championing both my words and my work over the years. May God continue to bless all that you do. As a result of your dedication and commitment, countless lives have been enriched, and the world is a better place.

Many people contributed helpful suggestions at various stages in the writing of this book. Some read every word and offered thoughtful guidance. In particular, I express my appreciation to these people: Rabbi Sam Gordon, who is a pioneer in the field of outreach to intermarried couples and their families; Jenny Jacoby of the Crown Family Foundation; Rabbi Dan Judson, a writing partner, colleague, and friend; Joan Peterson Littman, with whom I collaborated on *Making a Successful Jewish Interfaith Marriage;* and Laura Samberg-Faino, an important supporter of my work with interfaith couples and a member of the board of directors of JOI, the Jewish Outreach Institute. Laura read the entire manuscript; her keen insight, sensitivity, and many helpful suggestions are reflected in the pages of this book.

This volume would not have been possible without the guidance of Judith Schwartz, who served as development editor, and Emily Wichland, who is the managing editor at Jewish Lights Publishing. Emily has helped me in innumerable ways—on this project and on many others. In addition, some of the initial ideas for this book were shaped with the assistance of Elisheva Urbas, who has edited other writing projects of mine. I also want to thank Paul Golin, JOI's assistant executive director. It is his subtle genius as a wordsmith that makes so much of the work we do at JOI soar, including many of the ideas in this volume.

None of my work in the field would be possible without the support and encouragement of the board of directors of the Jewish Outreach Institute, my colleagues on staff at JOI, and the many families who share their lives with us on a daily basis. I also acknowledge with a profound sense of gratitude and abiding appreciation the creative leadership and unyielding support of Terry Elkes, JOI's president. I feel blessed to have him as my partner in this organizational enterprise and honored to call him my friend.

Finally, I thank my family—my wife, Sheryl, and our sons, Avi and Jesse—who support me, knowing how important this outreach work is to my rabbinate and how passionately committed I am to the task of promoting an inclusive Jewish community where all can feel welcome, regardless of the path that led them there. Each day they help me to reach higher while encouraging me to reach deeper into myself.

Introduction

Barukh haba. With these words I warmly welcome you. This Hebrew phrase, which basically means "we welcome you with blessing," indicates how wholeheartedly I welcome your interest in exploring Judaism and learning more about the Jewish faith and community. While some people approach Judaism curious to know exactly "what makes Jews and Judaism tick," this book is primarily designed for people whose quest to learn more about Judaism emerges mainly from a special relationship with someone who is Jewish. Perhaps your partner is Jewish, or your adult child or sibling. One way or other, the whys and hows of the Jewish religion have become personally relevant to you. What differentiates this from other introduction-to-Judaism books is the context and perspective on Judaism provided by an interfaith relationship.

Many books that offer a basic understanding of Judaism do so from a somewhat abstract point of view, conveying its tenets intellectually. This volume is not a "how-to" book of Jewish rites and rituals; it is more hands-on. For example, you may read about the Jewish value of, say, *tzedakah,* or charity, and then immediately have a chance to put that impulse into action within your family. Also, the examples used in this book will speak directly to you, the reader, as you too may have stood on the periphery of Jewish culture and are only now beginning to move into the inner circle of

Jewish life. Because of your circumstances, the issues presented in these pages are more relevant and thus more vivid for you.

As you will see, the questions implied by the information in this book are not merely theoretical or academic. Instead, they will lead you to insights on the religious and ethnic background of someone very important in your life. Your new knowledge may also help you understand your new relatives—an entire side of your new family whose customs, interests, and beliefs may have previously been foreign to you. If it is your adult child who is in a relationship with someone Jewish and he or she is now committed to establishing a Jewish home and raising Jewish children, then this book will provide a framework for the ideas and values that will help shape the moral character of your future grandchildren. This book will also give you a common language for family conversations, celebrations, and ceremonies. In addition, it will help the Jewish partner in a relationship to deepen knowledge about his or her faith.

Unlike partners who share the same religion, partners in interfaith relationships are often forced to ask themselves questions about faith and beliefs that they may not previously have reckoned with. As they navigate their relationship, an interfaith couple may feel the need to grapple in earnest with the material in this book; because of their differing backgrounds, such couples lack the luxury of taking beliefs and customs for granted. And they may want to discuss their responses and experiences with others. Thus, the book can serve as a resource for an even larger circle of people.

Many of the philosophical and practical matters considered in this book may come alive to Jewish people at various times in their lives. Interest in these issues may be sparked by special events or personal milestones, or may suddenly be made more compelling by a traumatic event in their lives or the lives of others in the community. For you, however, the particulars of this book may take on special meaning because of your interfaith relationship. You may feel as if you have to learn things about Judaism quickly, to catch up with born Jews, so to speak. Even though full understanding may require more time, study, or reflection, a familiarity with the concepts discussed in this book can make the difference between feeling part of an event and feeling uncomfortably alienated. But there is no substitute for the experience itself of holidays and religious services. These experiences will bring the reading and studying to life. They may also help to explain the rituals and general concepts, as well as the various nonreligious issues you will undoubtedly encounter.

Jewish spirituality includes religious beliefs, values, culture, and community. Because these are the cornerstones of Judaism, the book is divided accordingly into four chapters. Taken together, they offer a fairly well-rounded picture of Jewish life and living. Each of them is a valid entry point in its own right. Some Jews identify with Judaism in only one of the four ways specified in the chapters. Some people are motivated simply by religious beliefs, for example, and others by community. And that's OK. There is plenty of room along the continuum of Jewish life for those whose perspectives on the Jewish community differ in kind or in breadth. Knowing this might help you to understand some of the attitudes among your new family members that don't seem to make sense—for example, why Jewishness might be so important to those who don't actually practice the religion. This is probably the biggest disconnect about Judaism for non-Jews. While the Jewish religion takes a primary role in Judaism, there are many other aspects of Judaism. And many Jews relate to these other expressions of Jewish identity just as powerfully as their more observant brethren do. In fact, there are more Jews who are not affiliated with synagogues than those who are.

Judaism is generally defined as a religion, as opposed to a "peoplehood," particularly from the perspective of Christianity. Thus the first chapter of this book focuses on Jewish beliefs and religion. Your view of Judaism as a religion is most likely the same, regardless of your own religious background, whether you are Christian or Muslim or Hindu, whether your family's roots are in North America or Asia. Thus, this first chapter highlights hope and optimism as salient features in Jewish religious life.

Chapter 2 concerns core Jewish values, those that inform the actions Jews take and the decisions Jews make. Among other things, this chapter explains how the values of learning (*talmud torah*) and of good deeds (*gemilut chasadim*) underlie the way Jews engage with the world around them.

The third chapter spotlights Jewish culture. You can think of this as the more popular side of Judaism, life apart from religious practice and observance. This chapter details how Jews and others relate to various aspects of Jewish culture. It is about food and holidays, humor and ethnicity. It is about the lens through which the majority of Jews see Jewish culture, even if Jewish religion and places of worship constitute the more "official" view.

The last chapter of this book focuses on the Jewish community and its structures. Here I address the important role that Israel plays in the life of the Jewish people, as well as the inexplicable bond that many Jews feel with one another.

This volume is intended to be an introduction, presenting broad but key concepts of Judaism and addressing a selection of experiences you may encounter as someone new to the faith. I've outlined what I see as the basics you'll need to feel comfortable in many common settings; this involved making difficult decisions as to what to include and what to leave out. As your relationship evolves, you may encounter experiences not covered in this book, find scenarios detailed in these chapters that are not relevant to your life, or develop questions that are not answered here. So I have included "Next Steps" to help you move further along in your foray into Judaism, and at the end of the book you will find a list of resources to help you should you want to explore Judaism more deeply.

A NOTE ABOUT HEBREW

Most people associate Hebrew (particularly because it is the language spoken in Israel) and Yiddish (which is technically High German sprinkled with "loan words" from both Hebrew and the language of the country in which it was spoken, such as Polish) with Judaism. Though some readers may find Hebrew intimidating (particularly liturgical Hebrew, or Hebrew in the context of prayer), I have intentionally strewn various Hebrew (and sometimes Yiddish) words throughout the book. This is to familiarize you with the feel of the language and teach you the real meaning of the words.

Beyond its use as a contemporary language in Israel, Hebrew is also a sacred language. As such, it embodies many abstract Jewish values. Even simple words have complex meanings. The well-known *shalom,* for instance, means more than "peace." It refers to completeness or wholeness, a state of being that cannot be attained without peace. At first these words and concepts might be difficult to grasp, but learning them will pay off in the long run as you hear (and begin to use) them in your interaction with family and community. You will find these words gathered together in a glossary at the end of the book.

WE WELCOME YOU

The goal of this book is quite straightforward: to introduce you to the complexities of the Jewish religion and the Jewish faith in an accessible manner. This book fills a need created by the increasing number of interfaith marriages and the many Christians and others from different religions or cultures who are now making their homes within the Jewish community because of their relationships with people who are Jewish. While there are those in the Jewish community who see this as a problem, I regard it as an opportunity—an opportunity to share the depth and beauty of Jewish civilization with those who might otherwise not be exposed to it. Unfortunately, you may have received messages less than welcome from various people or institutions in the Jewish community. I acknowledge that—and quickly apologize for it. I want to make sure that you know how much I appreciate you and your interest in learning more about Judaism. So *barukh haba*—I heartily welcome you with blessings and introduce you, joined by the Jewish members in your family, to our faith and our community. May we all benefit from your presence with us.

1

Faith: A Constellation of Deeply Held Beliefs

Faith involves a commitment to an ideal, creed, or entity, and in many ways determines one's orientation to the world. In the Jewish faith, we devote ourselves to God. The way that Jewish people think of God and the place of God in our faith, however, is not monolithic. You may have already sensed that as a result of the encounters you have had with the Jewish community or the Jewish members of your new family. Throughout Jewish history, rabbis have grappled with the essential principles of the Jewish faith and the attributes of God. There is no single conceptualization of God, and Jewish scholars' attempts to define God are ongoing. So, while Jewish spirituality can be best understood within the context of a person's relationship with the Divine, the nature of that relationship varies greatly in contemporary Judaism. For those who practice other religions, such as

Christianity, where the nature of God is determined by doctrine, this might seem a bit odd. Indeed, you could ask many different Jews to explain their vision of God and get many different answers. The more you learn about the Jewish religion, the more sense this latitude of personal faith will make.

It is this latitude that puzzled Sean the first time we met in my office, shortly after he and Danielle began dating seriously. Danielle was frustrated that she couldn't answer most of Sean's questions about the Jewish view of God, which created tension in their relationship. She felt defensive: If she were asking him to accept her Judaism, she "darn well better be able to explain it." Perhaps she felt that his questions "showed up" her ignorance. So she turned to me for help. Usually, when I meet with couples, our conversation doesn't turn so quickly to God, but Danielle was determined. We jumped right into it. Not surprisingly, Danielle started with the conception of God that she had gleaned early in her religious education—something like an old man with a long beard. But it was clear that this was not the God of her Judaism, nor one that she accepted. Hers was more abstract, more powerful, but she hadn't given much thought to its resonance in Jewish tradition. After about an hour of deep, theological speculation, she felt a bit more relaxed when it became clear that some of her frustration in explaining her ideas about God to Sean emerged from Judaism's own multiplicity of beliefs.

Today's Jews talk more openly about matters of faith than did those of previous generations. There are more books written about it. The subject of faith in God appears more often in sermons and discussion groups, adult education courses and lectures. This reflects a larger cultural interest in spirituality that cuts across religions. Adherence to the Jewish faith generally involves belief in divine law, certain ideals, the value of life, and the importance of study and prayer. Belief in God—whether God is understood as an entity, a force, or a process—has provided spiritual and psychological grounding for hundreds of generations of Jews. To many Jews, God is something larger than us that unites us.

PRACTICE BEFORE FAITH

In Judaism, practice generally precedes faith and is usually considered more important. In many religions the "belief" part is considered most crucial; belief, in a sense, allows one to take part in other aspects of the religion. It's your ticket in. In Judaism it is just the opposite. What you *do* is most important; the faith will come. The shorthand for this is "deed over creed." I recall one woman who was raised as a Christian (her father was a minister) and had married a religious Jew. Though Maria had taken the conversion process seriously, she sometimes wondered whether her beliefs were authentic enough. Then she realized that this wasn't the point. She reflects: "For a while I would get frustrated with myself because I wanted my beliefs to drive what I did. But then I realized that as long as I prayed and observed with intention, the belief would follow. The faith comes with the doing." She had learned something on her own that I frequently have to teach others, since the Jewish model is counterintuitive to many people.

The nuances of faith and belief, and the ways in which faith and practice intertwine, may not be obvious as you observe the new members of your family. But understanding this can help you understand what they do and why they do it. In this chapter we will consider many questions about faith and its place in Judaism—questions that will be important to consider as your relationship with your Jewish partner and family members evolves.

SELECTED DATES IN JEWISH HISTORY

c. 1250 B.C.E.	Exodus from Egypt and settlement in the Land of Israel
c. 586 B.C.E.	Southern Kingdom of Judah destroyed by Assyria; First Temple in Jerusalem destroyed and the Jewish community exiled to Babylonia
c. 500–400 B.C.E.	The Torah, Five Books of Moses, is compiled/edited, according to biblical scholars
70 C.E.	Romans destroy Second Temple in Jerusalem
c. 200	The Mishnah is compiled
c. 300–600	The Babylonian and Palestinian Talmuds are compiled/edited
1178	Maimonides (1135–1204) compiles his code of Jewish law, the *Mishneh Torah*
1873, 1875	Reform Judaism in U.S. establishes the Union of American Hebrew Congregations and Hebrew Union College
1887	Conservative Judaism's Jewish Theological Seminary founded
1897	Theodor Herzl convenes First Zionist Congress
1933–1945	The Holocaust *(Shoah)*
1935	Mordechai Kaplan establishes the Jewish Reconstructionist Foundation, precursor to the Reconstructionist Federation
1948	Birth of the State of Israel

JUDAISM AS A PRACTICAL FAITH

As I explained, in Judaism *doing* is a precursor to *believing*. Therefore, Jewish faith can be understood as the sum total of what Jews do, both ritually and in their lives. It is true that people may engage in a ritual or take a particular moral position simply because "that's what Jews do" and they want to be in sync with Jews around the world or at least in their community. This is a commonplace explanation you will no doubt encounter as you try to learn about Jewish conduct. Typically, those who say this don't know the origin or meaning behind a particular practice or are simply mimicking what they have observed. When pushed, they might also say, "This is the way I have always done it." (Sometimes the copied behavior is incorrect, since they may simply be following someone who learned it incorrectly. This is particularly common in ritual activity.) Jews may not always be conscious of the various aspects of belief implicit in a particular ritual activity, like buying challah or flowers for Friday night or volunteering regularly at a local soup kitchen. Still, such habitual behaviors are revealing of Jewish faith. So in trying to understand Jewish faith, you can do no better than to note what people do.

The leeway in the way Judaism is practiced and, therefore, in the way Jews believe stems in part from the way the tenets of the faith have been passed down. A certain latitude is essentially built into the religion. Traditional Judaism asserts that the Torah (the first five books of the Bible, also called the Five Books of Moses) was revealed to the Jewish people by God through Moses on Mount Sinai. Thus it is considered divine in origin. While liberal Judaism may not accept the Torah as actually "written" by God, or even dictated to Moses by God (many liberal scholars would say that the Torah was "divinely inspired" or, as Reform Jewish theologian Rabbi Eugene Borowitz likes to suggest, that it is "the work of religious geniuses"), most regard the Sinai experience as the covenantal religious event, irrespective of its specifics. Regardless of the original source of the Torah, Jews on either end of the spectrum—and anywhere in between—regard the Torah as the *written* law, even if they disagree about the binding nature of that law.

According to rabbinic tradition, the transfer of Torah was not all that happened during the exchange that took place on the desert mountaintop: The so-called oral law was also given to Moses at Sinai. This spoken law was transmitted orally from teacher to student, from parent to child, from one generation to the next until it was written down in the Talmud many years later (c. 400 C.E.). With each generation, the law gained subtlety, commentary, and cross-commentary. It is this oral law, much more than the written law, that informs Jewish practice, Jewish belief, and daily Jewish living. And it is this oral law that is considered the source of rabbinic authority.

In a large sense, the oral model—even though it is now in written form—continues, as people continue to grapple with its meaning. My colleague Rabbi Bernard Zlotowitz tells me how much he has learned from studying his father's copy of the Talmud, which is filled with handwritten marginal notes, insights that his father gained while studying. This has become the "stuff" that the younger Rabbi Zlotowitz has taught his own children and students. You may find aspects of an oral tradition in your new Jewish family, particularly in the form of stories that have been passed down from one generation to another. Of course, this is not unique to the Jewish experience. It is only the texts and the contexts that make it so.

GOD IN THE BIBLE

The Torah has been called a story documenting the evolving relationship between God and the Jewish people in the ancient period. In modern times Jews have had a hard time talking about God until recently. Perhaps this relative dearth of discussion relates to Judaism's emphasis on action over belief. In other words, it may not matter to others what you think about God. Rather, what matters is how you act in relation to God. As a result, it is the action that is the focal point of any conversation. Or perhaps faith is considered more personal and private than ritual practice, much of which is public.

Anthony and Rebecca came to talk to me early in their relationship, and Rebecca was surprised when I turned the conversation toward God and belief. She felt that we should just talk about their relationship and things they might encounter when it came to children, parents, and the community—the last two of which were not being very welcoming to Anthony. She also admitted that she was not particularly comfortable talking about God, especially with a rabbi, since she really had not done so since she left religious school behind as a teenager. When I pushed her, she acknowledged that it was an area of intimacy that she and Anthony had yet to tackle and she was somewhat afraid to do so—since she knew little Jewish "Godtalk" and even less about what Christians said or thought about God. But once she started talking about what she actually believed, she became more comfortable. I reassured her that her perspective on God resonated with various strands of thought within Jewish tradition.

One can discern many aspects of God in Jewish liturgy— paternal, maternal (the term *Shekhinah* is often used in this regard), revelatory, redemptive, punitive. God is generally identified by divine attributes. These characteristics are emphasized by such names as "the Almighty," "the Merciful One," "Rock and Redeemer," and "the Truthful Judge." As noted in the Torah, the name of God should not be uttered directly, for God is ineffable.

Therefore, the Torah includes the so-called name of God as YHWH but the Rabbis assigned the euphemism *Adonai* (Lord) to be read whenever YHWH appears.

BELIEF IN GOD AS A STRUGGLE

In contrast to the Christian religion and many other faiths, Jewish faith in God is, virtually by design, an ongoing internal struggle. In Judaism there is no sense that belief in God brings immediate tranquility to the soul. Rather, according to Jewish spirituality, belief in God brings inner unrest. With such unrest comes strength of spirit and ultimately a deeper engagement with the Divine. This is a particularly unsettling notion to some Christians, even those who do not practice. To others it is a welcome and affirming response to their own experience of soul-searching.

As a model for this theological struggle, some rabbis turn to the scene in the biblical Book of Genesis where Jacob wrestles with an angel. The identity of this angel is not clear. Some say that it is really Jacob himself, or his own dark side. Others regard the struggle as between Jacob and God. As Jewish people, this is inevitably our own struggle. This idea is driven home by Jacob's being given the new name *Israel* as a result of the struggle. (The folk etymology for the name *Israel* is "the one who has wrestled with God.")

Every Jew's struggle with faith is marked by regularly questioning the existence of God and what we may call the actions of God. This includes challenging these actions outright. Rabbi Neil Gillman, who teaches philosophy and theology at the Jewish Theological Seminary in New York, the rabbinical training institution for the Conservative movement, likes to refer to this as "calling God out." I like to think of it as echoing the way the Jets called out the Sharks in the musical *West Side Story*. The Bible is filled with examples of its heroes challenging God. Early in Genesis, for example, Abraham spars with God over the potential destruction of Sodom and Gomorrah, cities whose people were identified as inherently evil. In the end Abraham loses and the cities are destroyed, but this is because Abraham could not find a sufficient number of righteous people there. As far as the logic of the story goes, had he done so, God would have spared the cities. The Rabbis later referred to such actions as *chutzpah clappei malah* (*chutzpah*—or guts and gumption—"in the face of heaven," that is, God). Abraham's words from that scene ring true for many of us when we learn of a tragedy or experience a tragedy ourselves. We may ask much the same question that Abraham did: "Will not the Judge of the earth deal justly?" (Genesis 18:25).

Moses, Jonah, and Job also have their brushes with God in the Bible. Perhaps challenging God is part of what turns a biblical personality into a hero; it's a spiritual rite of passage, so to speak. Regrettably, some people believe that struggling over faith in God—with its frustrations, doubts, and questions—makes it impossible to live a Jewish life, when in fact this is an important element of Judaism. Rabbi Levi Yitzchak of Berditchev made his mark on the community by virtue of his constant and public struggle with God. On one Yom Kippur, for example, he stood at the lectern in his synagogue and, raising his voice to God, said, "Our people come to You for forgiveness. It is not we who should ask for forgiveness. It is You who should ask forgiveness from us. I will not move from this place until You are willing to forgive us, and then we will do the same." His people learned that to challenge God was also to acknowledge a profound belief in God's influence in their lives.

I remember attending daily synagogue services with a colleague when I was studying for the rabbinate. Each day at synagogue I spoke the words of the liturgy, but he sat silent. At first I thought that he was uncomfortable or unfamiliar with the prayers or practices of that particular synagogue. Finally, I asked him, "Why do you go to the synagogue every day and say nothing?" He replied, "I am angry at God for how God is treating my mother." It turned out that his mother was suffering from cancer. While some might have expected this young rabbi to have prayed for his mother's health—a prayer for which I added to my own— he chose to express himself to God differently.

PROVING THE EXISTENCE OF GOD

Numerous rabbis and scholars have sought to prove the existence of God or to codify their belief system for others, but no one has been able to define God precisely. Some scholars have tried to make sense of God by offering their own understanding. Rationalists like Rabbi Leo Baeck argue that ethical monotheism is the essence of Judaism. Rabbi Baeck goes on to say that "the moral consciousness teaches about God." Mystics like Rabbi Adin Steinsaltz believe that there are four tightly related worlds, and the world we know is only one of a vast network of worlds. The specific world of Emanation is one of utter clarity and transparency, and so is identical with God; our goal is to come into complete— and mysterious—union with God, just short of what Zen Buddhists might call "the abdication of the soul" and what the Hasidim refer to as *devekus* (soul attachment, akin to the modern Hebrew word *devek,* "glue"). Those who regard God as transcendent believe that God is so distant and impersonal that one cannot speak to God directly; such a God is beyond human understanding and communication. To some, God's presence is immanent and one *can* relate to God directly. Others like Rabbi Mordechai Kaplan, founder of Jewish Reconstructionism, consider God as part of nature and are called pantheists. Still others think that the entire world is God; they are referred to as panantheists.

It seems that the more we try to say about God, the less we are actually saying. The medieval philosopher Moses Maimonides called this conundrum "the theory of negative attributes." Since Maimonides is such an important intellectual figure in the history of Judaism, you will encounter him throughout this volume. Trained as both a rabbi and a physician, he was a radical thinker who sought to repackage Jewish thought in a linear fashion to make it easily accessible to everyone and not the sole province of rabbis and intellectuals. Since Maimonides believed that the list of God's attributes was infinite, any attempt to enumerate them would always fall short. This reminds me of speakers who want to thank "everyone who made this event possible." Inevitably, someone who helped will be left off the list and be hurt by the omission. Thus, while the speaker attempts to enrich the experience of those who made the event possible, he is actually diminishing it for the one whose name is left off the list. In making a list of God's attributes, individuals usually note those things that they have experienced or observed or been taught. Ironically, while this may seem to increase one's understanding of God, it actually limits it, since the more we list about the Divine, the more we realize that there is much more to tell. Although it may not provide a satisfying clarity, most Jews have accepted Maimonides's notion of the futility of describing God. Maimonides resolved that the only way to describe God was, simply, as God. Nothing more and certainly nothing less.

THE NATURE OF GOD

In the Bible the salient image of God is as the creator of the universe. From the very start the biblical author frames this idea with the memorable phrase, "In the beginning, God created the heaven and the earth" (Genesis 1:1). There was no need for the Bible to say any more. For the biblical writer, the world itself was proof that God existed and clearly delineated God's role in the universe as creator and caretaker. Through the evolving biblical narrative, the author describes God as a surrogate, possessive parent of the patriarchs and matriarchs. God rewards those who do good and punishes those who transgress against the laws of the Torah. God also acts as guardian of the weak and guarantor of justice. When Moses asks God to disclose the divine nature, God's enigmatic response is *ehyeh asher ehyeh* (literally, "I will be what I will be"). When God describes the Divine Self as the creator, it is as if God were saying, "I will cause events to come into being [since that is essentially who I am]."

It isn't until chapters 33 and 34 of Exodus that the Bible attempts to speak to us directly about the nature of God. And the listing of divine attributes in Exodus 34:6–7 is not self-evident; it has to be interpreted if we are to understand it: "The Lord, Lord God is merciful and gracious, endlessly patient and abundant in goodness and truth, showing mercy to the thousandth generation, forgiving iniquity, transgression, and sin, and granting pardon." These attributes of God are chanted aloud in Hebrew in the synagogue prior to taking the Torah from the ark for public reading during festivals that fall on weekdays.

Even with the minimal amount of description of God in Exodus 34:6–7, the Bible establishes a foundation for the belief that a conception of God cannot be static. It evolves as our lives move forward. As we change, our relationship to the Divine inevitably changes. What remains unaltered is the covenantal relationship established between God and the Jewish people. It was this relationship that theologian Martin Buber described in his landmark work *I and Thou*. Buber suggests that all of our relationships should reflect the ideal relationship we are striving to establish with God. This means engaging at what he called the elevated "I-Thou" level, rather than the banal "I-It" level of the everyday.

For the Rabbis, the guiding principle concerning God is simple: God is one. All explanations derive from this idea. Some people call this notion the "unity principle." The ancient invocation *Shema Yisrael,* traditionally said during both morning and evening prayer services as well as before bed and finally just prior to a person's death, focuses on this core idea. Although this is usually regarded as a prayer, it is more of a sacred mantra (what is called a *kavannah,* or intention, in Hebrew), a spiritually evocative phrase that can be used for personal reflection as well as in the ritual of fixed prayer. If there is a difference between the biblical and rabbinic concepts of God, it lies in the Talmud's highly developed sense of God's openness to a relationship with the seeker, a nearness to those who pursue a relationship with the Divine. That is why I prefer to translate the *Shema* in a way that helps us understand this notion.

> *Shema Yisrael* (Listen, Israel—that includes all the Jewish people),
> *Adonai* (this is the personal, intimate aspect of God)
> *Eloheinu* (that personal God is connected to the distant awesome power of God that we experience in the universe, identified as *Eloheinu*),
> *Adonai echad* (they are one and the same).

MUST YOU HAVE FAITH TO BE JEWISH?

Those Jews most engaged in the Jewish religious enterprise— that is, those who belong to and support synagogues and other religious institutions—would probably argue that faith is an indispensable part of being Jewish. Yet the majority of Jews do not belong to synagogues. This contradiction puzzles many partners in interfaith relationships, particularly when Jewish families try to pressure their new soon-to-be relative to convert to Judaism.

When Katlin came to me confused about this very topic, I was not surprised. "Tell me," she asked rather sheepishly, "if the practice of Judaism is so important to my future in-laws, and they want me to convert and establish a Jewish home—whatever all that means—why is it that they do not even belong to a synagogue, let alone go to services? I am certain that I have never heard the word 'God' spoken in their home." This is a common experience for many Christians who enter Jewish families. The language that Jewish family members speak may sound religious, but it is actually ethnic. Yet its hold on the family is no less powerful. I explained to her that some families relate to Judaism through an ethnic identity that is manifest more in cultural than religious terms. Others hold onto fond religious memories from their youth that sustain them into adulthood and they want the same kinds of memories instilled in their children and grandchildren, although they don't realize that their participation is necessary for children to build those memories.

Your partner's parents may encourage you to join a synagogue even if they don't belong to one. While this may be difficult to understand, they are expressing concern that you and your partner maintain a Jewish family identity. They may look at going to a synagogue as the most tangible confirmation that their adult child intends to remain a Jew. They may not be expressing their intentions very well. And keep in mind that there are many ways to identify with the Jewish community. These will be discussed in depth in chapter 4.

For Jews who are religiously observant, regardless of where on the continuum of Jewish practice they fall, faith is a key element of their identity. And practice is intimately connected to developing a relationship with God. Of course, this is not the case for those, perhaps the majority, who don't relate to Judaism primarily through religion. Thus, while faith may be an indispensable part of Judaism for me, as for other religious Jews, this is not the case for everyone. For those completely outside the synagogue community or even those who are members of synagogues but rarely participate, faith may not be relevant to their daily lives. This isn't to say that these Jews do not believe in God or in a power greater than themselves. Rather, it means that faith and the practice of religion—in the way that traditional Judaism understands it—is not central to their Jewish identity.

DIFFERENT WAYS JEWS CONCEIVE OF GOD

While it is an overstatement to suggest there are as many ways Jews conceive of God as there are individual Jews, there is some truth to this notion. The Jewish conception of God can best be viewed as a continuum. On one end of the continuum are humanists like Rabbi Sherwin Wine, who hold the belief that there is no God (some, like theologian Richard Rubenstein, go as far as to say that the idea of God "died" in the Holocaust). On the other end are those who believe in what may be considered the fundamentalist Jewish concept of God as described in Jewish sacred literature (i.e., patriarchal, omniscient, omnipotent). I would say that for many, if not most Jews, the concept of God changes over the course of their lives. Sometimes these changes are rapid and global, incorporating various ideas simultaneously. For others, change evolves gradually over many years.

For example, while I have a general and fairly constant sense of what God is, my beliefs have shifted according to my experience with the Divine as well as my experience of living. Some of these events are major, like the birth of my children or the bouts of cancer that my wife has faced. At other times, events underlying a shift in my conception of God are subtle, as in the drift into middle age.

Most people who do believe in God hover somewhere in the middle of the continuum. Their conception of God may waver between one that is personal and immanent and with whom they can have a intimate relationship, and one that is impersonal and transcendent. Such variation is OK and does not diminish one's faith.

TENETS OF THE JEWISH FAITH

Amid all the variation, there are some general tenets of Judaism. Since there is no central Jewish authority—though many claim to speak as "the" Jewish authority—a loose consensus is the best we can hope for. Most of these core principles are related to God. Maimonides numbered thirteen essential beliefs related to God. Although all Jews may not agree with them, these tenets undergird the development of Jewish theology through the "additions" that the Rabbis made to biblical Judaism. Furthermore, this set of beliefs helps to make clear distinctions between Judaism and other religions, particularly Christianity.

God Exists

The first tenet is that God is the creator and ruler of all things. Arising out of this is the notion that God is eternal. Feminist theologians see this as a male perspective on God. They are concerned about the nomenclature used to describe God (King, Ruler, Sovereign) and argue that the idea that God rules the world just as a monarch rules a nation reflects the way men look at the world. When God is defined by these qualities, feminists feel as if they were viewing theology through a masculine lens. Feminist theologians look to define God in what they consider more maternal terms, focusing on compassion (in Hebrew, *rachmanut,* which is related to the word *rechem,* meaning "womb"). Nonetheless, what makes this perspective distinctive is that God rules over everything that God created. But God also shares that dominion with humans. Midrash (rabbinic interpretation of biblical stories) even considers the world unfinished after days of creation and suggests that one of the reasons that humans were created was to join God in completing creation.

Like the world, and unlike humans, the God who created the world is eternal (that is, immortal). Some scholars view the biblical story of the Garden of Eden, the eating of the forbidden fruit, and the expulsion from the Garden as a way of emphasizing this idea. Since the Bible reflects the human experience, Adam and Eve had to eat the forbidden fruit and gain specific knowledge. They learned that they were mortal. But they also learned that they could imitate God's immortality through the process of procreation—which they engaged in as a result of the knowledge they attained.

The idea that God is creator and ruler of the universe has come under fire over the last two generations, particularly since the Holocaust. If God "rules over" the world, goes the argument, then God should not have allowed six million Jews to perish during the Holocaust. In response, some theologians argue that God's power is limited and that God can't intervene in the daily affairs of the world. However, God is in a position to offer solace to those who have experienced pain and suffering. This is the view of Rabbi Harold Kushner, best known for his book *When Bad Things Happen to Good People.*

God Is a Complete and Total Unity

The second principle, according to Maimonides, is that there is nothing like God. God is sometimes referred to as the unique "unity principle." There is nothing that can even be compared to God.

God Is Not Physical and God's Presence Cannot Be Grasped by Human Imagination

For Maimonides the next important idea is that God does not have a body; God is pure spirit. As a result, the making of images of God is forbidden in Judaism. This notion is highlighted in the Ten Commandments. Nevertheless, in the Bible God is described in humanlike terms and expresses humanlike emotions, because people have no other terms with which to articulate their conception of God. This idea becomes a major point of contention between Jewish and Christian theology. While Christians argue that they also believe that God does not have a body, Jews find this difficult to square with the notion of Jesus. Historically, a number of sects were intrigued by Jesus, but they remained committed to practicing Judaism. Some even suggest that this is the model for the monastic Dead Sea sect known as the Essenes, as well as the Ebionites, the so-called historic Jewish-Christians (not to be confused with the contemporary "Jews for Jesus" groups). Eventually, Jewish practice by these groups diminished or was reconstituted as an independent Christianity emerged.

God Is Eternal and Prayer Should Be Directed to God

Not all of Maimonides's characterizations of God are self-evident or easy to understand. Among these somewhat cryptic divine traits are that God is the first and the last and that it is only proper to pray to God. Apparently, Maimonides wanted to emphasize the forever-ness of God. This suggests that God predates the existence of the world (as described in the Book of Genesis) and will exist after the end of the world as we know it (with the advent of the Messiah). Maimonides draws the conclusion that since God is the only God, and that God predates the world and will exist after the end of the world, it is fitting that this is the God to whom we should direct our prayers. Implicit in Maimonides's understanding is that humans would be predisposed to pray to God—once the authority of God were established and demonstrated.

God Communicates through the Prophets

Maimonides's next principle holds that because prophets are accepted as the spokespersons of God, all the words of the prophets are true. However, many of their prophecies are so ensconced in poetic language that they require a great deal of interpretation, which is then subject to debate among Jewish scholars. Liberal scholars, in particular, take issue with this claim, as they do with many others. If the divine origin of the Torah is called into question, so would any issue related to it, such as the "truth" of the prophecies contained in the Torah.

Moses's Prophecy Is Unique

In Judaism, Moses is considered the chief of all the prophets. Hence, Maimonides includes the acceptance of Moses as the leading prophet in his list of core principles. It is important to note that, even though Moses was the most important leader in Jewish history, particularly during the Exodus and the wandering in the desert, his role in sacred literature has been limited so as not to deify him.

The Entire Torah Is God-Given and Unchangeable

While most consider the Torah as the blueprint for the Jewish religion, Maimonides places this tenet toward the end of his list. Maimonides's principle suggests that the entire Torah that we now have, which was given to Moses on Mount Sinai, is exactly the way it was given; and states that the Torah will not be changed. Modern Jewish scholars have dealt with this idea differently. Some argue that the Rabbis indeed "changed" the Torah through their interpretation in the form of the oral law. Others suggest that oral law, given on Mount Sinai as well, merely helped to elucidate the principles contained in the written Torah. The various Jewish movements deal with this issue in different ways.

God Knows Our Thoughts and Deeds

God knows all of our thoughts. The idea of God as all-knowing runs through rabbinic literature. Maimonides considered this an important notion as well. This raises the question: If God is all-knowing and all-seeing, how can human beings have free will? The Rabbis suggest that these are not mutually exclusive postulates. They see God as knowing what decisions humans will make, without interfering with the process of that decision-making.

God Rewards and Punishes

God rewards those who keep the *mitzvot* and punishes those who transgress them. The framework of Jewish ritual observance and religious behaviors is marked by a system of commandments, or *mitzvot*. According to traditional Judaism, these commandments came directly from God or were interpreted as such by the Rabbis.

The Messiah Will Come

The Messiah will eventually come. The idea of a messiah comes straight out of rabbinic thought. Thus it is not surprising that some people have even gone as far as to say that Jesus was a rabbi. Where Judaism and Christianity came to differ on this idea— even before the specific ideas about Jesus as the messiah were codified by the Church—was on the question of whether the Messiah had yet come. Jews say no. Thus, for Jews, Jesus may have been a great teacher, even a prophet. But, according to Judaism, he was not the Messiah. Much of Jewish history and Jewish literature is informed by the Jewish notion of waiting for the Messiah. To take a contemporary example, there's a particularly poignant moment toward the end of *Fiddler on the Roof*. After the fictional town of Anatevka is destroyed by a pogrom, Tevye the Milkman says to the rabbi, "We have waited our entire lives for the coming of the Messiah. Wouldn't this be a good time for him to come?" The rabbi wistfully responds, "We'll just have to wait for him somewhere else."

We Will Live Again in the Messianic Era

The final notion introduced by the Rabbis and referenced by Maimonides is that of bodily resurrection. This is expressed as follows: "And the dead will be brought back to life." Judaism does not believe in the body's separation from the soul. The human being is a fusion of body and spirit. It is inconceivable for most of us to think of ourselves separate from our bodies. Thus, the notion of resurrection is really about the body being rejoined with the soul following the advent of the Messiah and the end of time as we know it (what is often referred to as the "End of Days"). This idea is not based in the Bible but emerges as a rabbinic concept, one that intentionally separated the Rabbis from the priests, whose religious lives were focused totally on the Temple. During the time of the Temple, the seat of community power rested with the priests—and remained there until the Second Temple was destroyed by the Romans in 70 C.E. However, Rabbis and nascent synagogues were emerging even while the Temple still stood. In order to wrestle community authority away from the priests, some upstart Rabbis identified a variety of concepts, including resurrection, that undermined many of the more limiting theological concepts held by the priesthood.

Practically speaking, this is why traditional Jews do not permit cremation. While many Reform rabbis discourage cremation of the body following death, Reform Judaism has historically rejected the notion of bodily resurrection. Therefore, the Reform movement officially allows for cremation. If you visit Israel, you may visit the Mount of Olives cemetery in Jerusalem, directly outside the walls of the Old City in the valley below the Temple Mount. This has been a popular burial site for Jews, because of the legends associated with the End of Days. Since, according to these beliefs, all will venture to Israel for final judgment, burying someone there makes the trip a lot shorter. This notion is behind many Jews' practice of placing a bag of dirt from Israel under the person's head in the casket before burial.

HOW HAS JEWISH FAITH ENDURED?

From the Jewish religious perspective, Jewish history is not simply the recording of events that have unfolded over time. Rather, Jewish history itself has a direction and a purpose, just as Judaism's function is to be a "light unto the nations." As a result, Jews have been sustained by a hopeful, meaningful vision of Jewish history even during its darkest periods. For example, there are many stories told about Jews who walked into the gas chambers chanting these words from one of Maimonides's Thirteen Principles of Faith: "I believe with perfect faith in the coming of the Messiah. And though Messiah may tarry, with all that, I still believe."

Religious practice is a reflection of Jewish faith. Ahad Ha-am, an early twentieth-century cultural Zionist, once remarked, "More than Israel has kept the Sabbath, the Sabbath has kept Israel." Ha-am meant that the faith implicit in the religious practices of the Jewish people helped sustain them throughout history. These practices—especially the "signature" practices of the Jewish faith, such as Sabbath observance—helped define who they are, what they believe in, and what they stand for. For the Sabbath, such practices include lighting candles, saying a blessing over the drinking of wine, and eating sweet challah bread.

COMMONALITY AND DIFFERENCE BETWEEN TWO FAITHS

Judaism and Christianity share the same roots. Thus Western civilization is often referred to as the Judeo-Christian tradition. While Christian religion argues that the "new covenant" established by Christianity obviates the covenant of Judaism as recorded in the Torah and explicated by the Rabbis, Jewish religion maintains the primacy of the covenant established with the Jewish people on Sinai. Nevertheless, Judaism and Christianity share many traditions that have their roots in folk religion. For example, both Christmas and Hanukkah are related to the winter solstice, the shortest, darkest day of the year. The reasoning is simple: When it is dark, you kindle lights. In Judaism's historical trajectory, these became the lights of the Hanukkah menorah by way of the menorah that was kept lit in the ancient Temple in Jerusalem. For Christianity, these lights became the lights on the Christmas tree, as well as those that adorn houses during the winter holiday season. Beyond this, Christmas and Hanukkah have little overlap because they have come to mark two unrelated events. Moreover, Christmas epitomizes the very essence of Christianity, in that it marks the birth of Jesus. It has thus become a shibboleth—*the* primary indicator used to measure the "religion" of a family.

Within a family, many people find commonality between the faiths through their own religious experience. Christine, who translated her Lutheran religious upbringing into Judaism, made sense of her new religious affiliation in this way. Though the symbols and holidays were different, she knew that she wanted to maintain the sense of God's presence in her family, albeit now a Jewish family. So she simply shifted from one to another. As in her own family, holidays were celebrated with both seriousness and lavishness. She now went to synagogue rather than church. She continued to pray regularly, but she now used a different prayer book. She sent her children to Sunday School at the local synagogue, just as she had been sent as a child to Sunday School at the local Lutheran church. While this sounds straightforward, she will be the first to admit that it was not easy. She mourned the loss of a certain part of herself for many years, especially the part that enjoyed the personal and particular Christian religious experiences, including going to church. However, she does not regret the choices she made for herself, her spouse, her children, and her family. She also admits that, since the frame of the religions were similar for her, she was able to gradually find meaning in Jewish practices. This helped her reconcile the various pulls that she felt inside herself.

IS "BELIEF" DIFFERENT THAN "BELONGING"?

For most Jews, Judaism is more about community—however loosely defined—than it is about religion per se, although belonging to a *religious* community is important to a large number of

Jews. When Judaism was primarily defined by religion (as opposed to culture or ethnicity) and Jews were forced to live within designated community boundaries, the notion of community took on particular significance. Belief sometimes leads to community. Jews who observe the Sabbath traditionally and therefore don't drive on the Sabbath must live within walking distance of the synagogue. This promotes closely knit Jewish neighborhoods and communities, which are found in most major cities: Squirrel Hill in Pittsburgh and Brookline in Boston, for example. But the notion of community itself, something required in order to experience belonging, is somewhat elusive in this postmodern world. Perhaps this is one reason why people are turning to belief first, as a route to a kind of community, and why many search for virtual community on the Internet.

THE ROLE OF THE DIVINE PRESENCE

If you were to ask the Jewish members of your family, they would probably say that Jewish faith is not possible without some acknowledgment of the Divine Presence—God. (Religious Jews often refer to this as *Shekhinah,* or God's indwelling presence. Because of the way Hebrew grammar works—*Shekhinah* is a "feminine" noun—many identify this as the feminine side of God.) For those who actively participate in Jewish ritual life, it is hard to imagine Jewish faith without a belief in God. Indeed, some manifestations of Jewish faith in God have stayed with Jewish people throughout history. Justice Louis Brandeis is reported to have said that what is remarkable about the Jewish people is not their ability to dream but their ability to realize their dreams. The believers among us would contend that God is at the source of this ability; others say that the will of the Jewish people underlies those accomplishments. Some say that will—exemplified by the hard work and perseverance of the early pioneers—caused the desert to bloom in Israel, while others suggest that was God at work. But everyone acknowledges the miraculous nature of what has been accomplished there. It is the record of these human achievements that often affirms the faith of individuals—regardless of whether or not someone deems God to be the source of these accomplishments.

THE IMPACT OF FEMINISM ON JUDAISM

The feminist movement has had a great impact on the Jewish community in general and on the liberal rabbinate in particular; many leading feminists have been Jewish women. In religious terms, however, the impact has been felt most keenly in the feminist conceptualization of God. Some people see this in the simplest of terms: sensitivity to the use of the pronoun *He* in reference to God.

Much of feminism's influence transcends the issue of pronouns and gets to the heart of the matter. In the Bible and throughout most of Jewish sacred literature, God is an all-powerful kinglike ruler, often referred to as *melekh malkhei hamlakhim*—king of the most kingly of kings. For feminists who see God as embodying other, more maternal qualities, such descriptions are too limiting. Some have even gone as far as to reconstruct the liturgy to address this issue. Thus, for example, God as King *(melekh)* becomes God as Source of Life *(m'kor chayyim)* or the Holy One of Blessing (from *Hakodesh Barukh Hu)*. This has indeed altered many people's conceptualization of God and opened people up to other options. Perhaps the most successful attempt to grapple with this idea is seen in the Reconstructionist movement's new prayer book. Rather than identifying God consistently with any pronoun or as King, liturgists have sought to understand which attribute of God is being expressed in the prayer and then identify God by that attribute. In one prayer, for example, God becomes the Merciful One. (There are several organizations—as well as many websites—that can provide you with resources on women in Judaism. A selection of resources can be found on pp. 141–148.)

OPTIMISM AND HOPE: EVER-PRESENT IN JEWISH LIFE

One of the greatest gifts Judaism has given the world is the message of undying hope. It is most eloquently expressed through the Passover holiday, which marks the ancient Israelites' liberation after four hundred years of slavery. In an attempt to emphasize that this message is woven into the fabric of the world itself, the Passover holiday is celebrated when winter gives itself over to spring, the most hopeful time of the year, and life itself is renewed. The biblical Exodus has become the prototype for the redemption from slavery of all enslaved peoples, including Jews during periods of oppression. To make sure that this story is remembered by all, it is retold during the Passover seder meal, the most universally celebrated of all Jewish rituals. Note: The telling of the story is the most important part of the holiday, not the eating of matzah nor the drinking of wine (both of which I encourage).

The possibility of redemption is a motif in Jewish life. It happened to our ancestors, so it could—and will—happen again to us, goes the logic. This idea of promise permeates Jewish liturgy and ritual, as it does all of Jewish life. For example, the *kiddush* blessing recited over wine, particularly on Shabbat and during holidays, cites the redemption from Egyptian slavery. Many interfaith families find that the observance of the Sabbath can be a "way in." They respond favorably to this notion of sacred time, a day different from the rest of the week, a time when all members of the family get together and separate themselves from the world around them.

Concretizing Abstract Ideas in Ritual Practice

All Jewish ritual practice takes abstract ideas and makes them tangible. We treat the Torah—where the story of the Jewish people and its ancient encounters with God is recorded—like a love letter from God to the Jewish people. And like a lover who receives such a letter, we read meaning into every part of it. We secure it in a special cabinet (the Holy Ark or *Aron haKodesh,* generally located in the front of the sanctuary in a synagogue). We handle it carefully and lovingly and take it out only on special occasions (such as when the community is gathered for Shabbat or holiday prayer), and then we honor it with a formal ceremony for the reading of it. We caress the Torah, holding it gently next to our hearts. We even kiss it, just to show how important it is to us, even as we recognize that its real value is in the ideas that the Torah contains. If our lover can't be physically present, then we can treat the words of love our lover has expressed as if they were our lover. And each year on the holiday of Simchat Torah, we even dance with the Torah, as if we were dancing with our lover.

The clearly orchestrated set of Jewish rituals—highlighted by study, individual meditation, and community prayer—provides the individual with a distinctly Jewish rhythm for living. When considered together, this array of rites, rituals, and prayer guides us through nearly every aspect of daily life and forms a unique spiritual discipline for the Jewish people to follow.

Study as a Complement to Prayer

Particularly with Jewish sacred literature, study is no mere intellectual pursuit. Rather, it is a powerful way to relate to God. So powerful that the Rabbis say that God is present when two Jews study. In comparing study to other ritual acts, the Rabbis say, "The study of Torah is equal to them all because it leads to them all." While most Christian study is focused on the Bible, Jewish study consists of the entire corpus of Jewish sacred literature, which encompasses such rabbinic literature as the Mishnah and the Talmud.

Though personal meditation as an isolated or routine spiritual practice is rather limited in mainstream Judaism, there are designated places for it in public and private prayer. For example, the so-called verses of song that are part of the fixed morning liturgy offer such an opportunity. While many rush through these selections from Psalms in order to get to the core of the service—and then on to the workday—they are designed so that the person praying can select a verse or two and focus attention on that verse. Even the text that introduces the core prayer (the *amidah*) in all three daily services is intended to be used as a meditation to help focus worshipers as they move out of community prayer and into private prayer while remaining in the context of the community. Some find the experience of *davenning* (a traditional approach to Jewish prayer with the back and forth swaying motion called *shuckling* in Yiddish) meditative.

PRAYER IN THE CONTEXT OF COMMUNITY

Community prayer is the preferred form of worship in Judaism. That is why, according to tradition, a prayer quorum, or *minyan,* is required for community prayer. Certain prayers cannot be said without a quorum of ten. Of particular note is the mourners' *kaddish* (the memorial prayer—though, interestingly, it makes no mention of death). This requirement may be seen as a way of encouraging the community to remember its obligation to those in its midst who are mourning and need their support.

Traditionally, Jews gather together for prayer three times a day (although the evening service is usually said immediately after the afternoon service). This is common practice among Orthodox Jews; it is less common for those who participate in other Jewish religious movements. If you live or work in an urban environment, you can probably join a daily *minyan*. Mourners (who are traditionally required to say the *kaddish* memorial prayer three times a day, once during each of the fixed services) may find themselves out of town—for Thanksgiving when visiting friends or relatives, for example. They will often look for a local synagogue, join a *minyan*, and be made to feel welcome. No questions asked. Some contemporary synagogues are often unable to assemble their members for such frequent worship. And some Jews, like myself, will often pray daily in private and only join the community for prayer on the Sabbath, holidays, and other special occasions.

Aside from holiday observances, those special occasions may include life-cycle events or community events. For example, following the cataclysmic terrorist attacks on the World Trade Center in New York, the Pentagon in Washington, D.C., and the plane crash in Pennsylvania on September 11, 2001, Jews flocked to their synagogues to be together, for we know that celebration is not enough. We gather together to express gratitude and thanksgiving, as we do when we are forced to confront unspeakable events that test our courage and even our imagination.

THE WELCOMING ENVIRONMENT OF SYNAGOGUES

Just because you are motivated to go to a synagogue or Jewish communal institution in response to a particular experience or event, it does not mean that such a place will be readily accessible. When we moved to our community twenty years ago, one of the first things we did was visit some of the local synagogues for worship services. We were attracted to the one closest to our home. That is where many of our new neighbors belonged as well. Unfortunately, we found the institution unwelcoming. On our first Friday night there, no one introduced themselves or even said hello. (Now the rabbi makes a point of encouraging members of the synagogue to reach out to unfamiliar people who are attending the service.) Furthermore, many religious institutions do not understand the barrier that their expectations of cultural literacy places on people, particularly those who are intermarried and lack the personal experience of Jewish memory. (I realize that your Jewish partner might be in the same predicament, but her lack of familiarity may go unnoticed, though that may be one of the reasons she has shied away from participating in Jewish communal religious life.) Expectations about ritual garb and even acceptable dress are made by synagogue members and seldom communicated to guests or newcomers. In one synagogue that I sometimes attend, the self-appointed usher asks each person he doesn't recognize, "Are you Jewish?" That is his unfortunate way of determining whether the person should be invited to put on a *tallit,* a prayer shawl. At the same institution, which has no assigned seats, guests are invited to sit in a specific section of the sanctuary so that they do not take the seats of regular attendees.

Synagogues should realize that there is a continuum of ritual practice within the community, with various entry points along the way. Not everyone enters at the same place. Besides creating a welcoming environment for you and your partner, I encourage synagogues to experiment with new rituals. As my teacher Rabbi Jakob Petuchowski used to point out, the rituals we regard as traditional today represent the innovations of a prior generation.

JEWS AS THE CHOSEN PEOPLE

When people hear the term *chosen people* in reference to the Jews, it makes them uncomfortable, thinking that it means "superior" or refers to those with "special privileges." For Bible readers, the sense is quite clear: "For you are a holy people to the Lord, your God, and God has chosen you to be a particular people to Godself, from among all nations that are on the face of the earth" (Deuteronomy 14:2). Yet the word *holy* really means "consecrated, set aside for a specific purpose." While some have argued that the term *chosen people* should be rephrased as *choosing people,* that is, those who choose the Jewish way of life and all that it implies, the notion of a *chosen people* refers to the responsibility of the Jewish people (chosen by God, according to tradition) to bring the teachings of the one God to a world that was decidedly pagan during Judaism's incipient years of formation. The chosen people are to be a "light unto the nations." Because Christians see themselves participating in that role on a Judeo-Christian continuum, the idea that Jews are a chosen people is one of the most difficult aspects of Jewish ideology for many to accept. Technical theological discussion is the province of theologians and does not impact the relationship of individuals, yet, on a religious plane, Roman Catholics see themselves as the "true Israel," thus supplanting the Jewish claim as the chosen people. This makes Jews rather uneasy. Likewise, the idea of *chosenness* is particularly hard for Christians in an interfaith relationship who feel excluded from some special realm—unable to ever access or approach it. In an era of political correctness, this is especially challenging to address.

To the prophets, Israel's chosenness meant that Jews had to shoulder heavier burdens of responsibility and meet more difficult standards of moral behavior. Failing to meet such standards provoked God to lead them into exile, according to the traditional understanding of the Babylonian exile in 586 B.C.E., when the first Temple fell, and then later once again in 70 C.E. These defeats led to the dispersion of Jews throughout the world. The Reform movement interpreted this dispersion (called Diaspora) in a more positive light, seeing it as part of God's plan for Israel to carry out its mission of disseminating the Jewish perspective on the relationship between humanity and God to the rest of the world.

Even those Jews who are not religious may readily accept the idea of "chosenness." The notion of chosenness was especially important during the dark days of Jewish history, when Jews needed this theological badge of courage, since it implies that God has a special relationship with the Jewish people.

The concept of chosenness emerged when God "chose" the Jewish people to receive the Torah on Mount Sinai and therefore enjoy a privileged relationship with God throughout history. By extension, this has been used to instill anti-Jewish attitudes by those who suggest that the Jews' chosenness implies that those who are not Jewish have an inferior relationship with God. All peoples have a distinctive relationship with God. The relationship of Jews with God is expressed in the Bible, which Christians and Muslims accept as the foundation of their own religions. However, medieval Jewish philosophers generally ignored the principle. It is not found in Maimonides's Thirteen Principles of Faith, for example, and Maimonides is considered to be the most influential classical Jewish theologian.

Understanding this challenge, the theologian Rabbi Mordechai Kaplan, founder of the Reconstructionist movement in Judaism, developed a theology that argued against the belief in such a relationship with God and removed from the liturgy all language related to chosenness. Changes in liturgy do not come easy for most Jewish movements. While there may be accretions in the prayer book, there are seldom deletions. Except for the few who accepted Kaplan's ideas without reservation, many Reconstructionist synagogues continue to use the traditional formulas for liturgy that include the notion of Jews as a chosen people—even as they transcend those formulas in most other ways. And although the Reform movement has debated the concept of chosenness from its understanding of historical Judaism, it has not sought to remove it from its liturgy. Instead, they reinterpreted it as part of its mission of ethical monotheism. Nonetheless, it is not something that occupies the daily discourse of most Jews, even those who regularly practice Judaism and who have left the language intact in the liturgy.

NEXT STEPS

1. Familiarize yourself with the synagogues in your community. Jews like to call this "*shul* shopping." Since *doing* is paramount, pay attention to how people act on their beliefs. You may want to take a look at the four major movements in American Jewry in chapter 4, pp. 116–120; which helps you grasp the difference between the various religious movements in Judaism.

2. Take a class or attend a program at the synagogue before you go to services. When you choose to attend services, you will already be somewhat familiar with the institution and some of its members. Holiday parties and celebrations, especially for young families, are often the best place to start.

3. If you are comfortable and interested, "try on" a Jewish ritual that is part of your partner's practice and that also feels right for you. Start simple. Don't worry about whether you are doing it correctly. All rituals take practice, and people get better at them in time. This is the best way to understand the power of Jewish ritual from the inside.

2

The Foundational Values of Judaism

As I discussed in the first chapter, understanding behaviors in Judaism is more pertinent than grasping principles of faith. This doesn't mean that beliefs aren't important. It just means that beliefs do not necessarily determine one's "Jewishness." Also, we can tell more about what people actually believe by what they *do* than by what they *say* they believe. However, behavior and faith alike are infused with values that have shaped the Jewish people throughout its history. Some of these values have grown out of the historical experience of the people and have become integral to Jewish culture over time. Other values have come directly through sacred texts, thereby claiming a divine source.

The very premise of this book derives from a specific Jewish value, that of "welcoming the stranger." While the English word *stranger* may be a little off-putting, the sentiments behind it are not. And there is probably no better way to translate the Hebrew term *ger* into English. (Interestingly, *ger* has been taken to refer to a convert to Judaism. When the word *toshav* is added to it to form the phrase *ger toshav,* it is often translated as "resident alien.") The logic is simple. Jews know all too well what it is like to be strangers or foreigners, immigrants or resident aliens, more or less welcomed newcomers in a land that they cannot call their own. As a result, once Jews are citizens of the land, they are welcoming to those who are "strangers." The instruction—"The stranger that lives with you shall be to you like the native, and you shall love him [or her] as yourself; for you were strangers in the land of Egypt" (Leviticus 19:34)—is so fundamental that it is repeated more than thirty times in various forms throughout the Torah. This is more often than any other individual instruction or commandment. Although we may think that Jews and Judaism are primarily concerned with matters like keeping the Sabbath and observing the dietary laws, the notion of welcoming the stranger is emphasized more. While you may not have yet experienced that sense of welcome—and one of the purposes of this volume, and, indeed, all my work, is to change that—it's "on the books" as a basic Jewish value. This value is so powerful that it drives the Jewish community, even in a period of history that has seen the Jewish community—in the United States, at least—far from being "strangers." At times we in the United States are lulled into forgetting that we were strangers, and thus we forget to welcome others. This remains true even as anti-Semitism rears its ugly head from time to time, reminding us of our "stranger" heritage.

Many core Jewish values add color and luster to the tapestry of Jewish life. Some of these values are made explicit in the prayer experience. The fixed prayers in Jewish worship services can be seen as expressions of the collective values of the Jewish people.

As Jewish values have evolved, so has the prayer liturgy. The introduction of the matriarchs into the prayer liturgy is one example.
The names of the patriarchs, or historical fathers—Abraham, Isaac,
and Jacob—have been part of our liturgy for centuries. In recent
years, with our increased awareness of the role of women in Jewish
life, liturgists have added the names of our historical mothers, or
matriarchs—Sarah, Rebecca, Rachel, and Leah. As Jews have
become more sensitive to the role of women in historical Judaism,
prayer book editors have sought to accord them their rightful place
in the context of the fixed prayer liturgy and the study of the Bible,
where historically their roles were either downplayed or overlooked
entirely. The idea is to integrate the values expressed by the liturgy
into one's life: One sings, chants, and meditates on such values as
being thankful for what one has, acknowledging wrongdoing, and
being united as a people, and then one acts on those values.
Likewise, one of the main reasons that individuals are encouraged
to join together in community for prayer, rather than praying
alone, is so that we can address community values as a community
of individuals brought together in common purpose. The sacred
drama of worship is designed to change behaviors through values.
And since the liturgy and rituals of worship have remained relatively constant (if anything, more has been added than taken out),
these values are passed from one generation to another.

Many aspects of Jewish life offer the chance to express Jewish
values. The specific values and the means by which they are
shared are explored in this chapter.

STUDY AND LEARNING AS SPIRITUAL EXPERIENCE

Especially since the time when the Rabbis took over communal
leadership from the priests, following the destruction of the
Second Temple in 70 C.E., Judaism has emphasized study and

learning. And the idealized Jew is a learned person. Take a look at most classical Jewish art: It is filled with people, often older Jewish men (it was, after all, done in a time before the recognition of women's rights and their important role in society), studying sacred texts. For Judaism, learning is not limited to formal schooling nor is it solely the province of children and young people. It is a lifetime endeavor. In my own case, when we moved to our current home I was more concerned about making sure that there was room for my books and a quiet place for me to study than I was about any other space in the house—including space for the television, stereo, and exercise equipment.

As students of Western civilization, we have a certain idea of what it means to acquire skills and knowledge in a particular field. We know that the American Jewish community is well educated, with more of its young people attending college than those of any other ethnic subgroup in the United States and Canada. Some might even cite the negative stereotype that Jews study and non-Jews play sports (the idea being that Jews are useless on the playing field)! Most likely, early in the relationship with your Jewish partner, someone suggested that you take an Introduction to Judaism course or read a book so that you could begin to learn about Judaism. Similar suggestions would undoubtedly be made in most religious cultures. However, it's particularly appropriate in the Jewish context because study is such a prominent feature in Judaism. It's not just a way for you to "know what we know" but also to "do what we do." As such, study can serve as a means of transition for you into a relationship with your Jewish partner and family.

Study in Judaism is far more than learning a collection of "how to's" about rituals or basic Jewish concepts. Of course, skills are important and knowledge of them will help you become accustomed to the Jewish community, particularly the Jewish religious community. But knowledge, even knowledge for its own sake (what in Hebrew is called *l'shma*), is valued as a route to something much deeper. We study as a way of getting closer to God. We study as a way of getting closer to one another. And we study as a means of getting closer to ourselves. I like to say that one does not study in order to learn more about the Torah, although this is what most people assume. Rather, one studies in order to learn more about oneself. And in the refracted divine light of Torah study, we are indeed able to see ourselves more clearly.

Study in Judaism begins with the study of sacred text as a spiritual experience. (Of course, the rationalists among us will simply study for the acquisition of cognitive information or exercise of the intellect.) For me and for Judaism as a belief system, study is a holy act—so much so that it is initiated with a blessing: "Praised are You, Sovereign of the universe, who makes us holy with *mitzvot* and instructs us to busy ourselves with the words— and works—of Torah." The reciting of this blessing is what makes such study different from any other kind of study. In addition, the morning service is marked by the study of brief selections of sacred literature. Public reading and study of Torah is a focal point of morning services for Shabbat and holidays, as well as services on Monday and Thursday mornings and on Saturday afternoons. Long ago, Mondays and Thursdays were market days, when people gathered in large numbers, so it seemed the most appropriate time to read Torah. Prayer provided the context and the appropriate atmosphere for the study of sacred texts, but the reading aloud of the story of the Jewish people in the form of the Torah took on greater significance. The reading and study of Torah was intentionally placed in the middle of the worship service.

When the Torah is read in public, this is supposed to reenact the experience at Mount Sinai, hence the ritualized choreography that surrounds the reading. So the group gathered around the study table where the Torah is read re-creates the scene when the ancient Israelites gathered around Mount Sinai.

So important was study that the Rabbis constructed a system so that people would not go more than two days without reading Torah. To augment the educational value of Torah reading and study, the Rabbis added the reading and study of *Haftarah* (readings from the Prophets and Writings, which came after the Torah in the order of the Jewish canon). Next came the addition of sermons and *divrei Torah* (short explanations or interpretations of the Torah reading). In many synagogues *divrei Torah* illuminate the themes and deeper meanings of Judaism for people unfamiliar with Torah study. This was true for Winston's late father-in-law. He had felt estranged from the Jewish faith until he joined a study group that met on Shabbat morning. He then started sharing *divrei Torah*; as a retired newspaper editor, the format of the study group—brief, thoughtful critiques and questions—suited him. For the first time in his life, he went to the synagogue every Saturday. Like him, you may find that listening to *divrei Torah* is a way to relate to the Jewish community. (There are easy-access resources now available on the Internet that are particularly helpful. Several are listed in the Resources for Further Study section, pp. 141–148.)

Torah commentaries are a product of Jewish history. Following the return of the Israelites from Babylonian exile, whenever the Torah was read publicly, a translator would usually translate the text from the Hebrew. This was particularly important because the general public had lost its familiarity with Hebrew around the time the Second Temple was destroyed in 70 C.E. These translations became explanations and interpretations, since "all translation is interpretation." Formats for public reading have changed slightly over the years, particularly in the pageantry that surrounds the actual reading. And people are now experimenting with various forms of interpretation, particularly in more liberal contexts. For example, with the ready availability of mass-produced translations, many synagogue congregations at do not read translations aloud. Instead, people are asked to follow along on their own as the Torah is being read in Hebrew. Some groups intentionally use a few different translations of the Torah so that the variety of translations and the differing interpretations become part of their exploration of Torah.

The Torah is the primary covenantal text in Judaism, so we study it as part of our affirmation of that covenant. Even though the Torah is routinely read aloud at synagogue, it is best to study it regularly on your own as well. Because of its origin (divinely inspired or written by God, depending on your perspective), its study emerges out of a relationship with God. This study takes a number of forms. The most basic is the *chevruta,* or study-partner model. (Modern pedagogues might refer to this idea as "cooperative learning," but it surely predates contemporary learning theory!) Contrary to what many of us were taught as children in secular schools ("Do your own work"), studying sacred literature with a partner is considered optimal. By studying with someone else, you are able to get the best out of your partner and out of yourself. Some people remain with the same study partners throughout their lives. Study partners form a microcosm of the community: Two people come together and build community, one pair at a time.

Other methods of study work just as well. Sometimes they take the standard form of classes, with a teacher providing guidance and direction. Or an informal group may get together regularly for self-directed study. Groups also form around specific themes, such as feminist study or the Torah as literature. Some people like to study on their own—or at least prepare on their own. They may appreciate the spiritual discipline of individual study or take it on as a personal challenge. For me, there is no better way to study sacred literature than with a study partner. It forces me to dig more deeply into the text and into myself, and allows me to help my study partner to do the same. While there are websites that offer guidance for finding study groups, the best place to find a study partner is among your friends. Most rabbis can offer suggestions, too.

Although Lizzie was raised as a Catholic, she was planning to marry a Jewish man. Once she came to a small study group held at the same time that her husband's children were in religious school on Sunday morning at the local synagogue. She had driven the kids that day and decided to check it out. The text of choice was *Pirkei Avot* ("Ethics of Our Ancestors"), an interesting collection of rabbinic aphorisms that offer wisdom for daily living. Because it is so insightful, *Pirkei Avot* is a very special text. It is also very accessible for most people. But what was most important for Lizzie was the group study experience. She surprised herself by how much she had to contribute. "Oh, I can get into this," she thought. Studying together with others in this way helped pave a path into the Jewish community for her.

The pursuit of learning becomes a spiritual discipline that helps to raise you above the everyday. Jeremy told me that immersion in sacred texts through study gave him the means to survive the pain following the death of his father. Such study provided him with a regular discipline when he thought the stability in his life had been undermined. Study became an anchor for him. With the regular companionship of a study partner, he was able to ease the soul-piercing loneliness that he felt after his father's death. Recognizing the divinity in the text helped him to realize that he was never truly alone and without support as long as he made himself aware of the constant presence of God. Through the study of sacred texts, he was able to gain perspective and move forward with his life.

While some cultures celebrate young people, Jewish culture has always celebrated old age, for with old age comes wisdom gained from the accumulated experiences of living. One of my favorite Yiddish expressions emphasizes this notion: *To the unlearned, old age is winter; to the learned, it is harvest time.* Judaism emphasizes lifelong learning, well into old age. It is clear that older students bring much more to the text than do younger students, who may be primarily interested in what they can get out of the text and not have much to add to it. According to tradition, some sacred texts should not even be studied by young people for this reason.

TZEDAKAH: AFFIRMING OUR PARTNERSHIP WITH GOD

In popular culture, there are plenty of negative stereotypes concerning Jews and money. Many of these emerged from the limitations placed on Jews in Europe during the Middle Ages. Because Jews were prohibited from most trades and crafts, many became moneylenders. This was a portable occupation that could take them across the borders of countries, should they be forced to flee. Many times in history, having money or gold has meant the difference between life and death. One rabbi tells the story that his father was sent off with gold coins sewn into his pocket so he could bribe the guards. Thus he escaped the Holocaust. Moneylending also permitted Jews access to places (in government, in particular) that would otherwise not be welcoming to them. But other people rejected members of the Jewish community because, as lenders, they held the pursestrings.

However, the relationship of Jews to money predates any negative Jewish stereotypes or animus toward the Jewish community as a result. The Jewish relationship to money has more to do with charity than anything else. Jewish tradition promotes charity in a distinct way. Even the Hebrew word for giving— *tzedakah*—translates more as "righteousness" than as "charity." *Tzedakah* is the Jewish means of redistributing wealth among people. Each individual, regardless of his socioeconomic status, is obligated to make donations to those less fortunate. In one respect this affirms the partnership between God and the Jewish people. God distributes the money, so to speak, and then Jews just redistribute it a little more equitably.

Of course, some see donating money as a form of flaunting one's wealth or trying to gain a measure of immortality (through the naming of buildings, university chairs, and the like). Charity can also be used to exert power and influence. If Jews appear to be overrepresented in the sphere of philanthropic giving, this may be viewed as a desire to sublimate the urge toward conspicuous consumption. But it's important to recognize that giving money and donating time have an ancient basis in Jewish values. Historically, Jews were discouraged from conspicuous consumption. In the Middle Ages rabbis tried to rein it in by issuing sumptuary laws. So instead of conspicuous consumption Jews have conspicuous *giving*!

Giving means a great deal more than simply parting with money. Through giving, Jews are taught to encourage the independence of others. Even the Hebrew term for possession— expressed as *yesh li*, literally, "it is to me"—indicates an awareness that ownership is time-limited. The Hebrew suggests that one is only in a temporary relationship with the object. Thus, it will not always belong to us; we are merely the stewards of our possessions.

Jews are called to support community institutions, as well as impoverished Jews and others throughout the world. *Tzedakah* thus becomes both a spiritual discipline and a *mitzvah* (divine instruction or command). The imperative to help others appears throughout the Torah and is explored by the Rabbis extensively in the Talmud. For example, those who harvest grains in the field are commanded not to harvest the corners of their fields or to pick up the gleanings of the harvest. Both are to be left for the poor, so that they can partake of the harvest and have food to eat. This form of giving is also built into Shabbat and each of the holidays. The notion of providing "flour money" to the poor for matzah on Pesach, for example, is as important as preparing one's home for the holiday. In my family, each week we empty the change from our pockets into *tzedakah* containers before making final preparations for Shabbat. (Some people refer to these *tzedakah* containers by their Yiddish name, *pushke.*) Because of the biblical origin of some of these ideas, they have found their way into Christian culture as well. Indeed, churches are well known for their acts of charity. While the specifics may differ, other cultures share in the religious desire to make the world a better place.

Maimonides, whom we have met in the first chapter, determined that there are eight levels of giving *tzedekah.* Whether they are aware of Maimonides's system or not, most people and institutions tend to use these tenets as guides in their giving. Maimonides was, above all, an astute observer of human nature.

Every act of giving is good regardless of its intent, but Maimonides believed that the nuances concerning charitable giving were crucial as well. They are listed below in increasing levels of "righteous giving."

The person who gives reluctantly and with regret.

The person who gives graciously but less than one should.

The person who gives what one should but only after being asked.

The person who gives before being asked.

The person who gives without knowing to whom one gives, although the recipient knows the identity of the donor.

The person who gives without making one's identity known.

The person who gives without knowing to whom one gives, and the recipient does not know from whom the gift has come.

The person who helps others to support themselves by a gift or a loan or by finding employment for them, thus helping them to become self-supporting.

There is one additional phenomenon that many Jews seem to obsess over: the recognition of donors. Honoring the donor has become a staple of Jewish fund raising. To the dismay of many, it has become woven into the fabric of Jewish communal life. Your first encounter with the Jewish community may even be at an event like an awards dinner or building dedication ceremony, with the top donors receiving star billing. If the Jewish family into which you are marrying is active in Jewish communal giving or in a particular community institution, you may encounter this on a regular basis. Jews may seem to obsess over this, yet there is a great deal of ambivalence surrounding the need to raise funds to support institutions that do good work and the recognition accorded donors in "over the top" ways. While many of us are looking for alternative approaches to fund raising, so that more funds can be spent on those who need it, remember that these activities do support the various organizations and institutions that benefit the community and beyond. One can argue that those who share their wealth with others deserve to be recognized for doing so. Some people who are new to the Jewish community, especially those who come from Christian churches that refrain from donor recognition, may be offended by this approach. To them it seems like an affirmation of the negative stereotype concerning Jews and money, or, at the very least, crass. Younger people, in particular, find this approach offensive or outmoded at best. Johnson, who did not have much experience with synagogues, told me that when he went into the synagogue for the first time, not realizing that the plaques on each seat were donor dedication plaques, he didn't know where to sit. Since there was a name plaque on each seat, they all seemed to be "assigned" to someone else. He would find a seat, sit down, and then notice that it "belonged" to someone. So he got up and moved to the next one. Eventually, not knowing what to do, he simply left the synagogue, assuming that since there were no unassigned seats that there was no room for new members!

GOOD DEEDS IN JEWISH TRADITION

Some people give their money. Others give of themselves. Still others are able to do both. The doing of good deeds (*gemilut chasadim* in Hebrew) complements acts of *tzedakah*. It provides heart to a somewhat complicated system of over six hundred commandments that Jews are required to carry out. (There are 613 to be precise, but don't worry. Many of these commandments are linked to the sacrificial system and ancient Temple cult and are therefore not required of anyone today.) Maimonides listed his version of the 613 commandments in a book called, appropriately, *The Book of Commandments*. These range from requirements for believing in God, to offering a *tamid* or daily sacrifice, to confessing sins before God and then repenting for them. Unlike *tzedakah*, which has a formalized system of measurement, the doing of good deeds knows no boundaries. There is no prescribed amount to be done. It is only required that we do them.

Central to the Jewish concept of good deeds is hospitality. The prizing of hospitality among Jews finds its roots in Abraham's welcoming stance as documented by the Bible. According to tradition, Abraham always kept the flaps of his tent open so that he could see visitors coming from all directions. Then he would rush to greet them and provide them with food and water, greatly appreciated by desert travelers. He would never wait to be asked.

The notion of righteousness underlies all the acts of *gemilut chasadim*. Certainly Judaism has no monopoly on good deeds. Most other religions and cultures require charitable acts, too. One action demands our special attention—the actions by Christians who saved Jews during the years of the Holocaust, throughout World War II. Many risked their lives to do so. They hid Jews in their homes and, as a result, put their entire families at risk. Many of these so-called "Righteous Gentiles" are celebrated in a special garden of trees at Yad Vashem, the Holocaust memorial in Israel. Oskar Schindler, whose heroic acts were portrayed in the movie *Schindler's List,* is one such Righteous Gentile.

The idea of Righteous Gentiles predates the Second World War by many centuries. The first Righteous Gentile was Pharaoh's daughter, who saved Moses from death under an edict issued by her father decreeing the destruction of all Jewish male infants. The Bible also mentions Shifrah and Puah, two midwives who refused to follow the edict and thus spared the lives of many Hebrew babies.

As a Christian, you may wonder: What is the difference between "being righteous" and "being saved"? Righteousness is not dependent on the acceptance of God (or as in the case of Christianity, Jesus). It is simply doing the right thing, doing good, for its own sake. Being saved denotes the whole process by which individuals are delivered into God's grace. In the Christian sense, this is dependent on knowledge of God and faith in Jesus. Such belief brings with it a forgiveness of sins. The love that is directed in return is a sign that the sins have been forgiven. But there is no such thing as "being saved" in Judaism. It is not that there is no Jewish notion of sanctity after death. Rather, it is not connected to our behavior in the same way that it is linked to actions in Christianity. Also, Jews do not believe that one has to maintain a specific religious belief (as in "accepting Jesus") to gain favor in God's eyes, or that one has to be Jewish at all. Personal redemption is not reserved for Jews. One is only required to follow the tenets of one's own faith.

THE EMPHASIS ON FAMILY IN JEWISH TRADITION

Plenty of ethnic groups value family, and each has its own, often endearing, often infuriating, means of expressing this. Jews certainly have their own brand of focus on family. In some respects, even the negative attitudes directed your way from members of your partner's family may be a reflection of this value. Because members of your partner's family fear that your marriage will dilute The Family, they want to protect it and they let you know it. It's best to help them understand that your marrying into the family can potentially enrich it, rather than diminish it. Many Jews experience Jewish continuity as an undifferentiated feeling of being part of an "in group." It is as if all Jews were one family. Some argue, as does Daniel Rushkoff, a contemporary social critic and the author of *Nothing Sacred,* that this stems from a sense of tribalism that is itself based on survival instincts. In other words, we feel close to those who are like us and bond with them immediately because this offers us a sense of security. We feel threatened by people who are not like us and therefore push them away. Jews seem clannish for both historical and scripture-based reasons. Throughout history Jews came under attack from other groups. So they cling together, even as they appear to fight among themselves over religious and community issues.

As for parental relationships, which may even seem smothering or codependent to some, this is enshrined in the Torah as one of the Ten Commandments: "Honor your father and your mother." Note that the Torah does not command us to love our parents, since it is impossible to love on command. Rather, the Torah instructs us to honor our parents (in Hebrew *kibud av va'em*). In the Talmud the Rabbis enumerate the dimensions of that respect, even when the relationships between parents and their adult children are strained and difficult, and even when—as sometimes happens—the parents have done things that led their children to withdraw their love. No matter what their parents do or who their parents are, children still have certain responsibilities toward them.

In practical terms, family relationships are nurtured in various ways. I know many families—even those who are not particularly religious or observant—who make it a point to spend nearly every Friday night together. Others get together for holiday meals (secular and Jewish) and for other kinds of celebrations. Conrad refers to Saturday as family day, meaning every week he and his siblings and their families converge on their parents' home for the day together. His wife confessed that, early on in their relationship, she found this overwhelming. Over the years she got used to it, and even looked forward to it from week to week. Now, as her children are getting older, she eagerly anticipates the same kinds of gatherings with them when they marry and have families of their own.

For some families, even simple life-cycle events (like a baby naming and a Bar or Bat Mitzvah) are by definition lavish family affairs. If you were not raised in such a family, you may find it extremely difficult to adjust to. Sarah, who is Jewish, was surprised at her husband's reaction when she told him that they were expected at Friday night dinners at her parents' home each week. She figured that he was used to Sunday dinners at *his* parents' home. He told her that his family had no such custom and that he would feel out of place at a Shabbat dinner. He felt more comfortable once assured that the dinner was about family more than it was an observance of Shabbat. Penelope, a Christian woman who married into a close-knit Jewish family, reported that the closeness of her spouse's family appealed to her. She had close Jewish friends growing up, and for her this practice had contributed to her decision to convert to Judaism, which she had made before she even met the man who became her husband.

Those who make family a priority place a significant emphasis on children and grandchildren. The fuss over children reflects a deep sense of renewal through the generations. This is particularly true in immigrant families where parents may not have had the opportunities now available to their children and grandchildren. In each generation parents want more for their children than they had themselves.

In Jewish tradition this may be expressed in concrete terms by a phrase used by parents in reference to a child. They may say something like, "This is my *kaddishel.*" This Yiddish expression comes from the name of the Hebrew prayer, *kaddish,* the memorial prayer for the dead, and implies that the designated *kaddishel* will be the one to say *kaddish* for a parent after the parent's death and thereby keep alive the parent's memory. You may hear this in families where there is no connection to traditional Jewish ritual; when dealing with the mysteries of death, in particular, people tend to return to practices that they themselves never observed. Often this practice leads the mourner to other Jewish practices and the spiritual discipline of a regimen of fixed daily prayer. This is another means of connecting to family.

Ruth, a Holocaust survivor, confided in me when she learned that her son had become engaged to a Christian woman. "I am not worried for myself. Nathan is my *kaddishel.* But I am worried for him. Who will say *kaddish* for my son when the time comes? Will he be able to raise a Jewish child to do so?" I suggested that she share her concerns with her son and his fiancée. The older woman's eyes welled with tears when she later related to me that her future daughter-in-law had put her mind at ease. She had said to the older woman, "Don't worry. I will be your *kaddishel* too. Nathan will not be alone. And I promise to bring children into the world who will be able to say *kaddish* long after we are all gone." It may sound morbid to talk about such things when people are so filled with life. But that is when these issues need to be talked about, when there is time to talk without pressure to act immediately, when it is not too late.

OUR CALL TO REPAIR THE WORLD

Hope, a sense of eternal optimism, permeates the Jewish holiday cycle, emerging explicitly in the Passover celebration, which takes place in the spring, and it suffuses all of Jewish life. It is reflected in the commitment to social activism and what is called *tikkun olam.* This term, which means the "repair of a broken world," is borrowed from the mystical Lurianic myth about the world shattering at creation and the scattering of holy sparks that need to be collected. Even among those who do not call themselves mystics or who are not followers of Isaac Luria or Kabbalah, this notion is central. The early Reform movement was built on the idea of social activism, the prophetic call to rebuild the world and the optimism that it is actually possible to do so. Reform Judaism did not rely on the messianic myth. Those who formulated this kind of Judaism rejected the notion of an individual who would become the Messiah. Instead, they felt that they could put their hands to work and rebuild the world themselves. While not dismissing the notion of a Messiah, other movements heeded the prophetic call to social justice as well. But the notion of *tikkun olam* transcends contemporary movements. It is woven into the fabric of social and ideological movements throughout Jewish history, such as the socialist movements of the late nineteenth and early twentieth centuries.

It is not surprising, therefore, that rabbis like Abraham Joshua Heschel walked arm in arm with civil rights leader Dr. Martin Luther King Jr. in Selma, Alabama, in the 1960s as a Jewish expression of conscience. Nor is it shocking to find that a large segment of the leadership and membership of organizations like the American Civil Liberties Union are Jews. Even the presence of Jews in historical movements such as communism and socialism is indicative of the ongoing Jewish commitment to fighting for justice in the world for all. The redistribution of wealth that we discussed previously as a form of justice stems from this same idea. Jewish history compels us to be liberators in concrete social and economic terms.

While *tikkun olam* may be seen as the expression of Jewish values in more secular terms, the idea of a Messiah (whether in the form of an individual or in terms of a Messianic Era) conveys this notion in purely religious terms. The belief that the Messiah will eventually come—and that the advent of the Messiah will mean an end of suffering for all—has kept the Jewish people alive throughout its long and painful history. Of course, false messiahs have garnered many followers, perhaps most notoriously Shabbatai Zvi in the seventeenth century. He proclaimed himself king and Messiah at a synagogue in Smyrna, Greece, in 1665. The people were seeking someone to make their lives easier, and the entire Jewish community was seized with a messianic fervor. Some even sold their homes and belongings in anticipation of their move to the Land of Israel. Following his imprisonment in Constantinople, Zvi converted to Islam to save his own life. Some of his followers still maintained their belief in him. Others rationalized the conversion as a descent into evil. The majority, however, evolved into groups that eventually broke away from the Jewish community entirely.

Belief in the Messiah finds its climax in the liturgy, at the end of the prayer known as *Aleynu,* which occurs near the conclusion of each worship service. The prayer is identified by this name because it is the first word of the prayer (that is fairly typical of the way the Rabbis named prayers and sections of the Torah read week to week), and the term *Aleynu* basically means "It is upon us." In other words, it is incumbent upon us; it is incumbent upon us to build a better world inspired by a divine vision. The conclusion contains an inspired and hopeful vision for a better world, which is encapsulated in the phrase, "On that day God will be one, and God's name with be one."

Historically speaking, Jews have found that the work of *tikkun olam* cannot be done alone. Thus Jews found community organizations. In general, the community is structured in two ways: religious organizations and secular organizations. The religious concerns of the community are usually regulated independently by individual rabbis and synagogues. Some cities have boards of rabbis, generally loose confederations with little authority. In the Orthodox community the rabbinical body *(Va'ad Harabbanim)* usually oversees the granting of individual kosher licenses (called *hekhsher*) for restaurants and kosher butcher shops. The more secular needs of the community are usually coordinated by a variety of social service agencies and organizations loosely affiliated with, and partially funded by, what is generically called the Jewish Federation. (Because of the history of individual communities, this central body may go by a different name in your area. Similarly, its national body has undergone various name changes.) While seeing itself as the primary voice for the Jewish community, particularly on matters related to Israel, the Federation raises money for local social service agencies, Jewish communities in need throughout the world, and Israel. While it is primarily a fund-raising arm, it has started sponsoring programs over the last generation.

But branches of the Federation do not work alone. Nor are they always successful in establishing themselves as the primary social services agency in a community. The Federation as a whole has been under attack by its detractors, many of whom were once its greatest supporters. In part, this stems from its reluctance to change its campaign message from "selling the Holocaust and Israel" to focusing more on the needs of the American Jewish community. In many communities, individual synagogues are more influential than the Federation and do a great deal more for the community. Just as synagogues are trying to renew themselves and become more responsive to the needs of the upcoming generations, the entire Federation is trying to redefine itself as well.

NEXT STEPS

Rather than taking a concrete step into the community, think first about the core values introduced in this chapter. For example, consider giving—your time and your money. And when you do, consider *how* you're giving—grudgingly or openly. Also, look around your community to see what you can do to make it better. My rule of thumb is simple: I only get involved if my involvement makes a difference. See who is doing *tikkun olam* work, even if they don't use that term to describe their efforts. Recognize that this is an expression of Jewish values.

3

Culture: Various Aspects of Jewish Civilization

WHAT IS JEWISH CULTURE?

It is difficult to define "Jewish culture" per se, because the lines that separate it from other aspects of Jewish life are rather blurry. Rabbi Mordechai Kaplan, the founder of the Reconstructionist movement in the 1930s, regarded Judaism itself as a civilization. To him, the Jewish "civilization" includes not only the religion but numerous cultural attributes, such as art, language, law, ethics, and even style of dress. For example, it may include certain aspects of holidays, such as food, but the religious dimension may be negligible. The ambience of the synagogue may be deemed "culture" but not the specific elements of community prayer. Culture is the taste of Judaism and its aroma, that which lends color and texture to Judaism but does not necessarily define it.

Arguably, more Jews embrace Jewish culture than Jewish religion. Culture demands no theological commitment, no synagogue membership, no adherence to hard and fast rules. It is the most tangible (including such things as challah and *hamantaschen,* for example) and yet, ironically, perhaps the most difficult for you to get your arms around. It is Jewish culture, in one form or another, that gives your new family its Jewish identity. Even if their knowledge of Judaism is limited, they have no synagogue affiliation, and they belong to no Jewish communal organizations, Jews may feel a connection with Jewish culture.

CULTURE VS. RELIGION: ARE THEY DIFFERENT?

Much of what we regard as culturally Jewish is, in fact, derived from religious life. For example, food like challah (the twisted egg bread traditionally used for Shabbat and other holidays) emerges from (1) the requirement to "sacrifice" a small amount of bread, as required by the ancient Temple cult and articulated in Jewish law, and (2) the braids of the Sabbath bride whom we symbolically welcome into our homes on Friday evening. Similarly, the view of Jewish cultural identity as intellectual comes from both the value of study and the biblical imperative to study. Even if you identify with Judaism culturally and not religiously, those cultural markers relate to the religion. Cultural Judaism is robust, even as many Jews are disconnected religiously. My colleague Rabbi Jennifer Krause believes that Jewish continuity is best understood as Jewish creativity. In her view, cultural activity is the only vehicle available for Jewish survival and growth—and renewal. Everything else that maintains the status quo leads us to stagnation.

Historically, there was little distinction made between Jewish religion and Jewish culture. For the most part Jewish religion was the route into Jewish culture. Only by reading backwards into history can we separate out Jewish culture from the ritual aspects of Jewish communal life. For example, while we might argue that Jewish religious rituals may not have been part of what has come to be called Jewish culture, the objects used to perform those rituals (especially when they were created by artisans) were surely integral to what has come to be called Jewish culture, such as *kiddush* cups for wine or spice boxes for the *havdalah* ceremony on Saturday night. Another example is Jewish folk music, which often takes its lead from liturgical texts and then finds its way back into the synagogue, although it was generally not composed for that purpose. Yet, even within the context of traditional Judaism, the cantorial arts are a designated Jewish cultural art form.

ETHNICITY'S IMPACT ON JEWISH CULTURE

By ethnicity, we mean a group that shares a cultural heritage defined by its language, customs, and history. Thinking of Judaism in terms of ethnicity allows us to talk about some sort of non-specific Judaism, a Judaism that is not necessarily defined by the Jewish religion—indeed, something that seems almost tribal in nature. No doubt it is this "ethnic" perspective that makes it so difficult for Christians to break into some Jewish families. A Jewish family's religious identification may be weak or nonexistent, but their ethnic identification with Judaism—however difficult it may be for them to articulate—is rock solid. It is not surprising that many people colloquially refer to fellow Jews as "members of the tribe," because that is how they feel about one another. And it can be argued that, historically, the Jewish people derived from clans or tribes.

While we may think of Jewish ethnicity as monolithic, it is actually multidimensional: Jewish communities around the world contribute threads to the tapestry of Jewish life. For example, the cultural life of Ashkenazi Jews, who descend from the Germanic lands, adds a distinctive dimension to Jewish culture that is very different from the Jewish culture created by Sephardi Jews, who descend from Spain and Portugal, or from the Asian and Arabic lands known as *Edot Hamizrach* (literally, "Eastern Lands"). The result is a variegated Jewish ethnicity with elements of each. If you come from one background, another tradition within Judaism may seem somewhat foreign to you. For example, rice is permitted to Sephardi Jews during Passover, whereas it is prohibited among Ashkenazi communities. And the recipes for Passover *charoset* differ as well, with Sephardim favoring the addition of dates to the "mortarlike" mixture.

The synagogues of Jews from these areas are generally distinctive as well. This runs all the way from the arrangement of the seats (courtroom-style for Ashkenazi Jews; king's throne room–style for Sephardi Jews) to the music used to chant the liturgy, which follows different tonal systems (referred to as *nusach*).

In some cases the ethnic culture of the communities and countries in which Jews lived throughout their history made such an impact on Jewish culture that it sometimes became synonymous with it. This is particularly the case with so-called Jewish foods, like corned beef or pastrami. But it also may mean that if you come from an ethnic background that bears some resemblance to what I described, you may have an easier time relating to your new Jewish family. So, for example, while Italian Catholics may not relate to Jews in terms of religion, they may mirror Jewish culture from the perspective of a close-knit family structure. This was demonstrated in the runaway hit movie *My Big Fat Greek Wedding*. Jews will tell you that they watched that movie and the family in it as if it were their own. The specific Greek details didn't affect their identification with the family at all.

AMERICAN JUDAISM IS UNIQUE

Contemporary American Judaism, inspired by American culture as much as by anything else, has developed a culture that is decidedly distinct from historical Judaism. For example, the notion of personal autonomy in Reform Judaism sprang from the democratic nature of America as well as the "me generation" of the 1980s. This is particularly noteworthy because most people think of Reform Judaism evolving from its German origins. While Reform Judaism is a movement that traces its roots to eighteenth-century Germany, the notion of personal autonomy was first articulated by contemporary liberal Jewish theologian Eugene Borowitz early in the 1950s.

In addition, American folk music, like the music of Peter, Paul, and Mary, or Pete Seeger, helped shape Jewish folk music, much of which is used in the synagogue liturgy today. Peter Yarrow's *Light One Candle* became a hit among Jewish kids as soon as it was released. Such music is truly grassroots, having found its way into the synagogue primarily through summer camps and youth groups. This is especially true of the music of Debbie Friedman, whose melodies are used in synagogues throughout the country. Adam Sandler's humorous "Hanukkah Song" stands as a shining, somewhat off-color, example of the influence of American culture, even if his word plays do not make it a favorite among Jewish educators or some parents. In Cantor Bruce Benson's "Jazz Service," the entire liturgy is delivered in jazz. As a result, it has a feel of being "uniquely American."

Other examples of the influence of American culture include the democratic governance of the modern American synagogue and the replacement of classic Jewish educational models with those pioneered by secular educators such as John Dewey. Dewey saw the school as a laboratory for learning and a training ground for students to learn the skills required to be adults in that particular society. Just about all the models still in place in American Jewish education reflect the ideas of Dewey and his disciplines at Columbia University in the early twentieth century. American Jewish educators applied his grade-leveled, textbook-focused classroom approach to Jewish education. This was crucial at a time when Jewish education in the United States was chaotic and cried out for order.

An indigenous Jewish culture in the United States did not emerge overnight. It can probably be traced to the Johnson Immigration Act of 1924, which placed limits on mass immigrations from Europe, including those of Jews. As immigration dwindled, the influence of the countries Jews came from fell as well. Jews in the United States no longer stayed exclusively in German-Jewish or European-Jewish enclaves. The fading of German influence in Reform Judaism began during this period. Early Reform prayer books were printed in German, and rabbis preached in German. This gave way to a preference for sermons delivered in English and the translation of prayers into English.

The recent focus on multiculturalism in the United States has renewed interest in other Jewish subcultures. The Haggadah that I prepared for children some years ago (*The Discovery Haggadah*) is filled with practices from other Jewish communities that I never encountered as a child; these are becoming increasingly popular. For example, some seders now feature the practice of Yemenite Jews symbolically beating participants with scallions as they walk around the seder table. In other seders, the *afikoman* is held for ransom by children rather than being hidden during the seder so that it can later be "found."

While there have been small peaks in the immigration numbers (following World War II, for example, or during the era of Soviet *glasnost*), the new groups have had little impact on American Jewish culture. The only outside influence exerting a force on American Judaism is Israel, most significantly following the Six Day War in 1967. This was seen in the surge in programs for students in Israel, the study of Hebrew, and the naming of children with Hebrew names, especially those that do not derive directly from the Bible. But even that influence in the shaping of American Jewish culture has declined significantly.

America is a *laissez-faire* society. Religion and religious identification are matters of choice. (Some people like to say that all American Jews are Jews by Choice, using the politically correct term for converts to Judaism.) People are neither forced to join nor forced to support Jewish institutions, as they once were in Europe. Like their counterparts in other subcultures, American Jews vote with their feet. And it is through this voting that American Jewish institutions and culture are shaped. Even the culture of the American synagogue is distinct. It does not look like the ancient synagogue or the synagogues of Europe that gave birth to most American Jewish communities. If anything, it reflects the American church as an institution. Although there are some noteworthy large synagogues, most began as small communal institutions that served the basic needs of the local communities. People went to pray and study. On occasion the synagogue was used either as a place of community assembly or as a refuge. As a result, it is not the differences in synagogue ideology that separate the synagogues from one another. Rather, it is the synagogue

culture that emerges from those divergent ideologies that underlies the difference between synagogues affiliated with the various
movements.

FOOD AS A LINK TO JEWISH IDENTITY

Food plays a big part in Jewish culture, particularly since eating is
as much about socializing, caregiving, status, and belonging as it
is about nourishment. There is very little in Jewish life that does
not include eating or food. Rather than expressing some sort of a
diet truism, the notion that "You are what you eat" communicates
the relationship between food and identity. This begins with
experiences Jews have as children. And although there may be a
learning curve with regard to food (you may have to develop a
taste for some Jewish foods, such as gefilte fish and horseradish),
it is much easier to scale this hurdle of entry into the Jewish community than other aspects of what I call the Jewish culture code.

But Jewish culture is about more than just food. Jews are generally more food-oriented than members of most Christian
denominations. In Judaism, specific foods and the way they are
handled are directly related to Jewish identity, especially in the historical context. Jews sought control over this aspect of life when
the Jewish people were powerless in so many others; this may have
prompted the stereotypical preoccupation with food and the
proverbial Jewish mother always saying, "Eat, eat!" It is also about
nurturing—such as taking care of oneself, expressing love for one
another, and affirming the value of life itself (as expressed through
good nutrition). Food—in the form of kosher dietary restrictions—
is a crucial aspect of Jewish segregation, of keeping separate from
other people. It has also been a core element in holiday celebrations. There is a rich menu of foods associated with most Jewish
holidays, such as *hamentaschen* for Purim and *latkes* for Hanukkah.

As much as they have an independent identity, they also serve as symbols for the holidays—Hanukkah just wouldn't be Hanukkah without *latkes*. Preparing (and eating) *latkes* creates sensory memories. This is particularly important for children to carry into adulthood and eventually try to re-create for their own children. The focus of most Sabbath celebrations on Friday evening is around the dinner table, where the table is transformed into a "small sanctuary," replacing the ancient Temple altar, rather than the synagogue and its prayer service.

The culture of food extends beyond the food itself. In my home, for example, the only time we eat in the dining room is on Shabbat and Jewish holidays. Even when we entertain guests on other occasions, we generally eat in the kitchen, largely because it seems homier and more friendly. But for times when we want to raise the mundane to the sacred, eating in the dining room seems to provide a more appropriate setting. Once when my children were younger, we went to visit some friends who were not Jewish. When they invited us into the dining room for a meal, my older son, Avi—maybe he was four or five at the time—said to me, "I thought you said that the Arnolds weren't Jewish." "They're not," I replied. His response was, "Then why are we eating in the dining room?"

Kashrut—Understanding Jewish Dietary Laws

The Jewish dietary laws, called *kashrut*, have had a great influence on Jewish culinary culture. These laws are intended to emphasize the sanctity of life and a rigorous spiritual discipline by focusing on three basic areas: the proper slaughter of animals and their preparation for consumption; permitted and prohibited foods; and the prohibition against mixing milk and meat, which is extended to include fowl. Thus, it can be said that there are three different aspects of *kashrut*. Some will argue that the primary purpose of the Jewish dietary laws is to keep Jews from socializing with non-Jews. In the ancient world this meant the separation of Israelites from idol-worshipers, presumably because early Jews were vulnerable to their influences. If we dig more deeply, we find that what may have been feared was that socializing could lead to intermarriage (although, in fact, the Bible is filled with numerous examples of successful intermarriages).

Others will argue—incorrectly in my opinion—that health and hygiene provided the primary rationale for the fundamental laws of *kashrut*. Ritual washing before eating may have staved off the spread of plagues in Europe among the Jewish people, but its purpose arose simply out of the desire to protect oneself from ritual impurities. And while the improper preparation of pork products can lead to trichinosis, the Rabbis were clearly unaware and uninterested in health as a reason for the observance of *kashrut*. As they understood it, these were laws from God, and that is what motivated their regulations.

Regardless of the rationale, if the laws are scrupulously observed they may limit the interaction between Jews and non-Jews. Ironically, in the American embrace of food culture (where so-called Jewish foods such as bagels, chicken soup, and chopped liver have become staples), non-Jews often seek out Jewish foods. For example, the kosher dairy restaurant near my office, where I often eat lunch, is frequented by people of various backgrounds. It is a kosher restaurant that happens to serve good food and thus attracts a wide-ranging clientele.

HOLIDAYS EXPRESS VALUES OF THE JEWISH PEOPLE

The holidays dominate religious culture. For people in sync with the holiday seasons, the seasons bring different moods. The fall holidays—Rosh Hashanah, Yom Kippur, Sukkot, Simchat Torah—introduce us to a season of personal reflection and repentance. If someone speaks ill of someone else or repeats some gossip, people may remark about its inappropriateness during the season. In our home we hurry to complete major purchases or repairs before the fall and spring holidays, in anticipation of entertaining more guests and visitors than during other times of the year. It also feels right. When I led a large suburban synagogue in West Hartford, Connecticut, I could always tell the weeks that preceded holidays. Every member of the staff worked hard to make sure that the building sparkled. Brass was polished, windows and carpets cleaned, floors waxed, offices straightened up.

For those who really embrace the Jewish holidays, the fall season may be overwhelming. And with so much time off work, it is hard to get things done (maybe that is the point, to focus our attention on the important things rather than what usually occupies our attention). Recently, someone who had married into a Jewish family asked me quite innocently, "Why are there so many holidays bunched together in September and October when you can go weeks for a time without a Jewish holiday?" She expected a rational answer but there is none. I had nothing to say except, "It is sometimes a pain in the neck. But if you jump in with both feet, you will learn to enjoy them as I do." It may not have been the answer she was looking for, but I certainly have come to enjoy the holidays and luxuriate in them—even though they can seem a bit much to take on.

Although holidays could be discussed in any chapter of this book, I chose to introduce them within the context of culture because I think holidays inform and shape Jewish culture. While rabbis may speak of holidays in religious terms, we observe them as family occasions—in much the same way as we celebrate the

Fourth of July or Thanksgiving. Thus, they make a significant contribution to our understanding and appreciation of Jewish culture.

You will quickly observe, if you haven't already, that Jewish holidays never seem to fall on the same date from year to year. The joke is that they are either early or late but never on time. While the secular calendar is solar—that is, governed by the sun—the Jewish calendar is soli-lunar—governed by both the sun and the moon. Thus, while the dates may change somewhat from year to year, the holidays always occur around the same time of year. These dates are fixed according to a complicated formula devised by the Rabbis many years ago. In order to follow the cycle of Jewish holidays, you should have a copy of the Jewish calendar or a secular calendar that includes Jewish holidays as well. On pp. 129–130 you will find an at-a-glance summary of the major Jewish holidays and the approximate times of the year they occur.

Holidays serve as markers on the Jewish calendar as we travel through the year. We know, for example, that the summer is over and fall is close at hand when we ready ourselves for the High Holidays: Rosh Hashanah and Yom Kippur. Holidays also serve as historical markers, raising historical events to a sacred level. Hanukkah, for example, celebrates the defeat of the Syrian-Greeks and their sympathizers, and the rededication of the ancient Temple in Jerusalem. Contemporary holidays have historical resonance, too, such as Yom Hashoah, which recalls the Holocaust and the memory of all those who perished at the hands of the Nazis. Holidays and observances are part of our identity as Jews. Even those who may not think of themselves as particularly Jewish may feel compelled to take part in holiday events. We feel a visceral connection to them, and in this way the holidays serve as reminders. Chris shared with me this example. He was caught up in the rush of a multiday business trip and noted that the hotel where he was staying displayed the Israeli flag. Puzzled, he asked the front desk clerk about it. The response: "We have lots of visitors to our city (New York) from Israel, and it is Israel's Independence Day. So we fly the flag out of respect and support." My friend, who had married a Jewish woman only months before, was overwhelmed by the goose bumps that were raised upon hearing the clerk's explanation. He had the same experience when he told me the story.

MAJOR JEWISH HOLIDAYS

Perhaps more than anything else, Jewish holidays express the spiritual and emotional values of the Jewish people. Some say that, when considered together, the holidays evoke the entire spectrum of human emotions, as well as the Jewish values that are integral to Jewish religion. During the holidays these values reveal themselves in concrete ways. The holidays below are organized not in calendar order but in the order in which they are regularly and most frequently observed by the majority of North American Jews, particularly those who are not affiliated with a synagogue. Shabbat is first because it occurs weekly, even though it may be observed with regularity less frequently than other holidays.

Shabbat

While Shabbat is not technically a "holiday," many of the holidays share a great deal in common with Shabbat, especially with regard to traditional Jewish law. It's a kind of template for all Jewish holidays, and in fact Shabbat "trumps" all other holidays. Its laws generally take precedence over the laws that govern other holidays. Beginning each Friday evening, an hour before sunset, Shabbat provides us with an opportunity each week to separate ourselves from the workday world. It concludes twenty-five hours later at sunset the following day, officially when three stars can be seen in the sky. Through resting we are able to renew ourselves in preparation for the week ahead.

Shabbat is ushered in in style. We dress up the table with a tablecloth and our best china. We light candles, eat the special braided egg bread called challah and drink wine—all with the appropriate blessings. The cup of wine is to be full to overflowing; such is the abundance we feel on this day. Then we eat a festive family meal. On one end of the observance continuum, people speak of the "spirit of Shabbat" and do those things that seem restful and relaxing to them—even if they are not prescribed by traditional Jewish law. These might include a leisurely drive "in the country," participation in a sporting event, or attending a musical concert or dance performance. On the opposite end are those who observe Shabbat through the strict application of Jewish law. Thus, they do not do anything that may rob Shabbat of its sanctity. The prohibitions are derived from the labors associated with the building of the Temple in ancient Jerusalem. They have been translated into the modern era to include a prohibition on driving and the use of electricity (for some, this even includes turning on household lights). Business transactions are not allowed on Shabbat. The challenge for all those who observe Shabbat is to navigate their way between the spirit and the letter of the law.

The synagogue observance of Shabbat includes an extensive fixed liturgy highlighted by preselected readings from the Torah and *Haftarah* as well as Saturday afternoon study. It is also a time to visit with friends, family, and fellow synagogue-goers. While some people may focus on the prohibitions—what you can't do—the Sabbath is a joyous occasion. Mystics say that observance of Shabbat offers us a foretaste of the "World to Come," that time and place imagined by the Rabbis that was to follow the coming of the Messiah.

Shabbat may be a powerful experience for anyone, especially those new to the Jewish community, whether or not you have chosen to convert to Judaism. There is nothing more liberating than being forced to stop working at the approach of sunset on Friday evening until nightfall on Saturday night. Mathilda, a recent convert to Judaism, told me that Shabbat has served as a regular reminder of her entrance into the Jewish community. She says that she does one new thing each week in recognition of it. Sometimes it is as simple as a new recipe for the Friday evening meal, which she enjoys preparing more than any meal during the week.

Passover

Passover is a festival that occurs in the spring and celebrates the Exodus from Egypt and the redemption of the Israelites from Egyptian slavery. It is one of three pilgrimage festivals—the other two being Sukkot and Shavuot—so named because Jews historically made a pilgrimage to the ancient Temple in Jerusalem for these holidays. The Passover story begins with a request made by Moses to Pharaoh on behalf of the Jewish people to leave Egypt temporarily in order to celebrate some kind of springtime festival. This ancient festival was eventually integrated with what has come to be known as the holiday of Passover. It is observed by more American Jews in one form or another than any other holiday on the Jewish calendar. Perhaps this is because it is primarily a home-based, family-centered holiday, thus unencumbered by Jewish communal institutions. Families get together for a structured family meal (called a *seder,* meaning "order") that tells the story of the Exodus through a well-orchestrated guide called the

Haggadah (literally, "the telling of the story"). The most powerful and liberating aspect of the entire holiday is its message of freedom and hope, and the eternal optimism that permeates it. Matzah, the humble unleavened bread that is the salient element associated with Passover, becomes a symbol of hope.

Some people like to think of Jesus's Last Supper as a Passover seder, but New Testament scholar Rabbi Michael Cook, who teaches at Hebrew Union College–Jewish Institute of Religion in Cincinnati, suggests that this is not so. Even in the New Testament there is disagreement about whether or not Jesus's last meal was indeed a Passover seder. Paul described it as an ordinary meal. Mark, who wrote later than Paul, considered it a Passover meal, but John, who writes even later, suggests that the Passover meal took place on the Friday night following Jesus's crucifixion.

It wasn't until after the Temple was destroyed and there was no opportunity to sacrifice the paschal lamb—as required by the Torah—that the seder as home ritual became a standard Jewish practice. Prior to the Temple's destruction in 70 C.E., Jews ate matzah and *maror* (bitter herbs) and told the story of the Exodus and the sacrifice of the lamb, but there was no complex step-by-step seder meal as we know it. The seder, replete with prayers, songs, and stories, did not develop until almost fifty years later. This replaced the Temple sacrifice and gave the Jewish community a meaningful narrative to comfort Jews suffering from the loss of the Temple. The seder grew out of the simple instruction of Rabban Gamliel (c. 90 C.E.), who explained the three basic symbols of Passover: matzah, *maror,* and the *pesach* (alternatively called the *zeroah,* the shankbone, symbolizing the Passover offering). While it is popular for churches today to celebrate a Passover seder, and while it is an excellent opportunity for Christians to learn about Jews and Jewish observance, the seder is best understood as a Jewish ritual that developed among Jews, following the parting of the ways of Christianity from Judaism.

Because Passover and Easter take place in the same season, sometimes with overlapping days, some intermarried couples feel a tension during this period. Some interfaith families try to blend Passover and Easter, but like most attempts to draw parallels between holidays from divergent traditions, the result is somewhat superficial. Easter and Passover may share some of the same historical roots (emanating out of a springtime folk festival that celebrates fertility and rebirth), but they are inherently different. Families end up with all the trappings and none of the deeply moving religious experiences for which each of these holidays is known.

I remember one interfaith family, the Hendersons, who tried to encourage the celebration of both holidays. They sent their young daughter, Michelle, to an Easter egg hunt during Passover with the warning, "You can go on the hunt, but you can't eat any of the candy since it isn't kosher for Passover." Needless to say, this instruction made little sense to their daughter. Along with her parents, Michelle soon learned that if she were to fully celebrate one holiday, she would have to let go of the other. So the Hendersons celebrated Passover at home and simply acknowledged Easter with grandparents when celebrating the Christian holiday at their home.

The emphasis of Passover is on storytelling—the retelling of the story of the Exodus. This makes it a perfect opportunity to invite Christian members of your family to learn more about the Judaism of the family into which you have entered. While most of the people sitting around our seder table each year clearly know the story of Passover, we intentionally invite people for whom the story is new. I always enjoy seeing the reactions of our guests as the story unfolds. One year, upon leaving the seder, Gwen, a

Christian guest, told me, "I now understand things about Judaism and the Jewish people that I never realized before. Now I know why so many of my Jewish friends act the way they do. Optimism in the face of adversity provides a foundation for all that you do."

Hanukkah

Hanukkah marks the victory of a small band of Israelites over the large Assyrian-Greek army in 165 B.C.E. The renegade Israelite army, organized by Judah the Maccabee and his brothers, did everything they could to win, including using guerilla tactics. However, the text from the prophet Zechariah reminds us of the core value expressed in the holiday: "'Not by power, nor by might, but by My spirit,' says *Adonai*" (Zechariah 4:6). While many focus on the military victory, it was the *spiritual* victory of the Maccabees that offered cause for celebration. The Rabbis emphasize this as they retell the story of the Hanukkah "miracle." According to legend, the Maccabees returned to the ancient Temple in Jerusalem and found it in disrepair. Following its cleanup, they sought to rekindle the menorah that adorned its walls. Alas, they found but one flask of consecrated oil among the debris, enough for only one day. They knew that it would take days before they could consecrate additional oil for the dedication of the Temple. However, the oil lasted for eight days (coincidentally the same amount of time it took to dedicate the Temple). For me, the real miracle is that the Israelites regained religious freedom and self-governance. The actual length of time that the consecrated oil burned is almost irrelevant. Once it—and their religious fervor—was rekindled, it burned far beyond the length of time the fuel made possible.

However, this holiday is not just about a struggle with enemies from the outside. It is also about insiders who embraced Hellenistic culture and welcomed its influence on Jewish culture.

These were fellow Jews who embraced the Assyrian-Greeks and their presence in Israel. So Hanukkah celebrates the struggle and victory of purists or pietists over assimilationists. While the purists won, the struggle continues. There's a constant tension among members of the Jewish community as to how much of the outside culture should be absorbed and taken as our own. The fatal battle of the original Hanukkah is eclipsed by the greater victory of the Maccabees. Similarly, in our day some of the conflict between the various segments of the Jewish community is eclipsed by the struggle for Jewish survival in America, in Israel, and abroad.

The first Hanukkah (165 B.C.E.) was actually a celebration of the fall harvest festival of Sukkot, which could not be observed because the ancient Israelites were denied access to the Temple in Jerusalem. They had no intention of creating a new holiday. Before Sukkot could be celebrated, the Temple had to be dedicated. Hence, the name Hanukkah, or rededication, and the eight days' duration.

The spinning top (*dreidel* in Yiddish, *s'vivon* in Hebrew) is one of Hanukkah's key symbols. The toy is probably an adaptation of a gambling game. On each *dreidel* are written four Hebrew letters—נגהש—one per side. These stand for the four words: A "Great Miracle Happened There" (*Nes Gadol Hayah Sham*), a reference to the miraculous victory of the Maccabees. In Israel the inscription of the *dreidel* is slightly different—נגהפ—with a one-letter change: A "Great Miracle Happened *Here*" (*Nes Gadol Hayah Po*). Given how small the world really is and the impact of the Hanukkah experience on the entire Jewish community, I have never found the need for two different *dreidels*. The Israeli version works fine for me.

Hanukkah is associated with two other items: a menorah or *hanukkiyah* (candelabra that contains space for eight candles or oil reservoirs, plus one to do the lighting), and foods made with oil, usually *latkes* (potato pancakes) and fried jelly doughnuts. The menorah is borrowed from the seven-branched menorah that was housed in the ancient Temple. An additional branch and service candle are added for the ritual of candle-lighting at Hanukkah.

Many members of the Jewish community see Hanukkah as the defining issue in the life of an interfaith family. In other words, whether a family celebrates Hanukkah or Christmas or attempts to celebrate both lies at the core of its religious identity. Like Christmas, Hanukkah has its roots in ancient folk religions celebrating the winter solstice as the turning point in the season. But the commonality ends there. While I am not in favor of Christmas trees in Jewish homes, I know that life is about compromise. Each family has to figure out what works best for them, making sure that what they do represents both who they really are and what they want to communicate to their children, the outside world, and themselves. It can be a tense season for many families, which is why it is often referred to as the December Dilemma.

Purim

Purim, a late winter/early spring carnival festival, is based on the story of the plot to annihilate the Jews of ancient Persia that is told in the biblical Book of Esther. This plot was conceived by Haman, a member of the king's court, and was foiled by Mordecai, a nobleman, and his niece Esther, who became queen to King Ahashuerus. Esther used her position in the king's harem to persuade the king to thwart Haman's evil scheme.

The Jewish people prevailed once again and are thankful for it. Thus, Purim is an expression of unmitigated joy for having survived. This holiday is pure fun, a time to truly let loose. (It shares a lot in common with Mardi Gras.) Just about everything in

Purim works backwards, including the festive meal, which ushers out the holiday rather than welcoming it in. This is just one way that the festival pokes fun at some of the solemnity of Jewish rituals. Even the regularly scheduled daily services are parodied. For example, prayers are sung to the melodies of popular music. Historically, one was encouraged to drink until "you cannot tell the difference between 'Blessed be Mordecai' and 'Cursed be Haman.'" With today's contemporary sensitivities toward alcohol abuse and addiction, many synagogues and communal institutions have played down this aspect of the celebration. It is also popular for children to dress up as the characters in the Purim story and perform skits that play out the tale.

There are few ritual items connected to Purim—only noise-makers and the Scroll of Esther—but one food stands out as a Purim treat, *hamantaschen* (*oznei-Haman,* "Haman's ears," in Hebrew). These are triangular, filled pastries. Scholars differ on their origin. Many say the name is a Yiddish pun on Haman and *man* (poppy) and *taschen* (pockets), and that the shape represents Haman's hat or his ears. Some will go as far as to say that since Purim takes place in the spring, it has roots in folk religion and spring fertility rites.

Sukkot

Each agricultural harvest season in Israel has its festival, and Sukkot is the one designated for fall. It comes fast on the heels of the High Holidays. According to tradition, as soon as people break the fast for Yom Kippur they are supposed to begin the construction of their *sukkah,* the temporary booth used to celebrate this festival. These booths represent the portable dwellings that the Israelites used during their journey in the desert from Egypt to Israel. They also reflect the shacks built by harvesters in the fields, where they would periodically rest, since it would be a waste of daylight to go back and forth from the fields to their homes. I never fully appreciated this notion until I spent a month on an Israeli kibbutz during the apple harvest season. We arose in the morning before daylight, worked for several hours following sunrise, stopped for breakfast, worked several more hours, rested a bit, and worked still more hours before stopping for the day when the midday sun was the most intense. When we took a break out of the sun we used primitive shacks we had built out of the debris from the harvest: branches, leaves, and other natural "litter" that would eventually find its way back into the earth.

During Sukkot our home is filled with guests invited to join us in the *sukkah* for each meal. Because the emphasis is on family and food and a break from our everyday settings, this holiday provides an excellent opportunity to "test out" Judaism or introduce Judaism to other family members. According to the talmudic Rabbis, understanding Sukkot is crucial to understanding the historical journey of the Jewish people. And short of the ritual bath, the *sukkah* provides us with the only full-bodied Jewish experience. Perhaps because he was trained as a carpenter and was much handier with tools than were many of my friends, Tom quickly became a *sukkah* construction expert. This despite the fact that he was new to the Jewish community—having only married Ilene a few years before.

Shavuot

This late spring harvest festival marks the giving of the Torah to the Jewish people on Mount Sinai and celebrates the first fruits of the season. The first yield—or first fruits (*bikkurim* in Hebrew)—in a harvest is considered to be the best. With the passing of time, Shavuot became more of a celebration of God's revelation and less a celebration of the harvest. Some synagogues invite new babies for blessing in the synagogue during this holiday—their parents' "first fruits."

The most interesting custom associated with Shavuot, which has enjoyed a renaissance of late, is the gathering for all-night study called *tikkun layl Shavuot*. People study various texts, often from rabbinic literature, that deal with the revelation of Torah or the benefit of studying it. Then at sunrise, those who had been studying gather together for traditional morning prayers. Because the holiday is associated with the giving of the Torah, which coincided with the specifying of the Jewish dietary laws, only dairy and *pareve* (neutral) products are eaten on Shavuot.

In Reform and some Conservative synagogues, confirmation ceremonies are held on Shavuot. This is an example of a ritual openly borrowed from Protestant Christianity. Congregations celebrate their children as the "first fruits" of their labors while the children confirm their commitment to the Jewish faith. While the ages for confirmation may vary, confirmation generally takes place once young people have completed tenth grade and are at the end of their formal religious school training, although some continue studies into eleventh and twelfth grades.

I have found that *tikkun layl Shavuot* is an excellent entry point for newcomers, especially since few adult Jews in liberal communities have a memory of this experience. Thus, newcomers can join in to create a shared memory with members of the Jewish community. It is a powerful emotional and community-building experience to spend the night together studying.

Tu Bishevat

Not one of the big holidays, Tu Bishevat (Jewish Arbor Day) is often referred to as the "birthday of the trees." It recognizes the beginning of spring renewal, near the end of the rainy season in Israel. It has become a Jewish Earth Day of sorts, with a focus on the land and the environment intermingled with a celebration of the Land of Israel. Its simplicity is what speaks so loudly about this holiday that emphasizes nature and its source. Planting trees and shrubs, and nurturing them as they grow through the years, is an extraordinarily rewarding activity.

More recently, the mystic tradition of a special seder for Tu Bishevat has gained new adherents in the Jewish community. While it borrows some of its order from Passover, it is really more of a fruit and wine-tasting event. Like some of the other minor festivals, there is no fixed liturgy and no hurdles over which Christians have to climb in order to celebrate with Jewish members of their family.

Yom Hashoah

Yom Hashoah is the day designated to mark the Holocaust and memorialize its victims. It is among the newest of Jewish holidays and observances on the calendar. While there is no formal liturgy for Yom Hashoah, communities generally use the occasion for public presentations and memorial services. Often survivors are invited to address the gatherings. Dramatic presentations, musical performances, films, and art exhibits may be offered. This observance is an example of the evolving nature of Jewish civilization and culture. As history moves forward and we continue to confront it, there are events that require our attention and deserve recognition in the ritual and religious calendar.

Of special note are the cultural contributions of those who perished in the Holocaust, as well as those who survived. They have become part of the Jewish cultural "canon." Some, like the works of author and witness Elie Wiesel and *The Diary of Anne*

Frank, have transcended the Jewish experience and become hall-marks of American and world culture.

Yom Ha'atzmaut

The festival of Israel Independence Day celebrates the birth of the modern State of Israel. In Israel, its observance looks a lot like the Fourth of July in the United States, with flags, fireworks, and picnics. There is a great deal of debate in synagogue circles as to what special prayers should be added to the formal liturgy, but the real celebration takes place in the streets, in parks and audi-toriums, and in people's backyards. The holiday is observed in late spring on the anniversary of the day that Israel declared itself an independent state (May 14, 1948). It takes place one week after Yom Hashoah and one day following Yom Hazikaron (Israel's Memorial Day). On Yom Hazikaron those who gave their lives in defense of Israel are mourned. This includes resis-tance fighters as well as those who have fallen victim to terror-ism. Yom Ha'atzmaut is usually marked in the United States with rallies supporting Israel or with Jewish community fairs that cel-ebrate Israel.

SYNAGOGUE: THE CORNERSTONE OF JEWISH CULTURE

While the majority of Jews are not active participants in the Jewish community, the synagogue still seems to be the corner-stone of the Jewish community. When people move to a new city and want to know the Jewish lay of the land—where the Jewish neighborhoods are, the best kosher deli, and so on, they usually go first to the local synagogue. Synagogues from each of the movements in Judaism vary from community to com-munity. However, in most communities, except for those that are exceptionally small, it is common to find Reform,

Conservative, and Orthodox synagogues, most of which will be identified by the national movements with which they are affiliated.

Many people distinguish among the various movements as if they represented set points on a scale of Jewish observance. Even though Orthodox Jews are more likely to observe more traditional Jewish practices than Reform Jews, what truly differentiates the movements is the ideology that underlies particular observances. For example, Orthodox Jews understand their obligations as commanded by God, articulated in the revealed law of the Torah, and interpreted by the Rabbis. They believe that they have no choice. Reform Jews, on the other hand, believe that they can exercise a great deal of personal autonomy in their personal pattern of observance because they do not accept the Torah and its foundation of law as divinely revealed, but rather, as the work of humans, inspired by God.

The social and political positions taken by members of the various movements generally reflect their position on observance. For example, the Reform and Reconstructionist movements openly welcome gays and lesbians into their communities, and many of their rabbis will officiate at gay and lesbian commitment ceremonies. They admit and ordain gays and lesbians in the rabbinate. The Reform movement was also the first to ordain women as rabbis and open up synagogue ritual and leadership to them, allowing women to read publicly from the Torah and sit as presidents of congregations. The majority of Conservative synagogues have followed suit. Orthodox Judaism still resists these changes, although women have made considerable strides in the Orthodox community in the last decade as well.

You may find synagogues to be "high-barrier institutions," difficult to access from the outside. This is particularly true when a Jewish partner is also uncomfortable with synagogues and thus can't be much of a tour guide. Reform and Reconstructionist synagogues may generally be more welcoming to interfaith families than are Conservative and Orthodox synagogues, but don't be misled by labels. Far more important is how you and your partner and your children are *really* welcomed than the affiliation of the synagogue. Just as education depends on the teacher in the individual classroom and not the school itself, some rabbis and some congregations are simply warmer and friendlier, no matter what their affiliation.

The synagogue as an institution is undergoing change, aided by a variety of national projects like Synagogue 2000 and STAR (Synagogue Transformation and Renewal). However, the synagogue remains the bedrock of the Jewish community. People are glad that the synagogue is there, even if they are its greatest critics and even if they step inside only for the High Holidays. When I was a congregational rabbi, the members of the synagogue spoke proudly of their synagogue and its impressive physical presence. They liked identifying themselves to others as members of that synagogue. They would recall with fondness the exact spot where they stood to be blessed as a married couple or where their baby was named or their child celebrated a Bar or Bat Mitzvah. And many loved every single brick in the building and had the same kind of feeling for their synagogue that people have when they think of their childhood homes or neighborhoods.

LIFE-CYCLE EVENTS CONNECT COMMUNITY

Jews mark time in a variety of ways. Over the course of one's lifetime, milestone events are made special through ceremony and religious observance. This begins with birth and proceeds through death. In most respects Judaism is not unique in this regard. However, Judaism devotes more attention to the end of life than its beginning. That is why, according to Jewish tradition, families traditionally recognize the anniversary of a loved one's death, called *yahrzeit*, rather than his or her birthday after the person has died. Life-cycle events are excellent opportunities for people to connect or reconnect with the Jewish community. Sometimes this stems from a spiritual need. It is common, for example, for someone to take on the obligation of saying *kaddish* (the memorial prayer) after a parent has died, after having had little or no relationship to the synagogue or formal institutional Judaism for many years. The routine of saying *kaddish* within a *minyan* (prayer quorum) at the synagogue helps create a significant bond, one that is not easily broken at the end of the required year of mourning.

Ceremonies for Babies

There are several ceremonies for babies, depending on the community and the sex of the child. Most people are familiar with the ritual circumcision that takes place on the eighth day of a male child's life. In Jewish tradition, this *bris* or *brit milah* ("covenant of circumcision," in Hebrew) as the procedure is called, is performed by a *mohel*, someone skilled in circumcision and knowledgeable in Jewish ritual law. In communities where there is only one *mohel* or a particularly popular one, the *mohel* becomes part of the culture of the community. For example, one *mohel* is known to have "done" most of Chicago. And, of course, circumcision jokes have entered popular American culture by way of Jewish culture. From the perspective of Jewish law, if the mother is Jewish it will be easier to find a traditional *mohel* willing to officiate at the *bris* (or *brit milah*) of a male child born to an interfaith couple than if the father is Jewish and the mother Christian.

In the latter case, probably only a *mohel* trained by the Reform movement will agree to officiate. Male babies are named at the time of the *bris*. Girls are often named later, at a ceremony in the synagogue or in some cases at ceremonies that parallel the traditional *bris*. Such events usher girls into the covenant with symbolic acts, such as the "drinking" of wine, being swaddled in a *tallit* (prayer shawl), or washing the feet.

Bar/Bat Mitzvah

This ceremony, held when a child turns thirteen, marks the formal transition from childhood into adulthood. The traditional age for this transition for girls is twelve—some synagogues will hold *B'not Mitzvah* (plural of Bat Mitzvah) for girls following their twelfth birthday—but many girls celebrate their Bat Mitzvah at thirteen just as boys do. The ceremony as we know it dates from the medieval period, and though there are many challenges to the integrity of this ritual, particularly as it is observed in the American synagogue, it remains an important one. Children make important steps toward maturity during their preparation for a Bar or Bat Mitzvah. For many, this is the first time that they have to prepare extensively to make a presentation before a large crowd of adults. While they may not truly become "adults" in the contemporary sense, they now take on the religious obligations of adulthood and can be included as an adult as far as ritual requirements are concerned. They grow through the process and so do their relationships with their parents and their community.

Some synagogues pose many hurdles for interfaith families to overcome in order for Christian members of the family to be included in the ceremony. For example, some will allow non-Jewish family members to ascend the pulpit but not accept any so-called pulpit honors, those activities that guide the flow of the service, such as opening and closing the holy ark, but that do not require the recitation of any formulaic blessings. Others will allow parents to address the child and the congregation. Some think this has to do with Jewish law and its parameters, but it is really about the culture of the individual synagogue and how inclusive it chooses to be.

The Bar Mitzvah ceremony used to be simple: The young person was called to the Torah to recite the blessing before and after it was read. It remains relatively simple in some communities today. Originally, the Bar Mitzvah was a marker of time, in the same way that the right to vote or to purchase alcohol is reached at a particular age, whether or not one acts on that right. Today, however, B'nai Mitzvah (plural of Bar Mitzvah) have become elaborate affairs, often competing with weddings in expense and lavishness. People may want to outdo their neighbors, so we hear about one family renting the *Queen Elizabeth II* and another renting the Gator Bowl. In my congregation we tried to control the level of conspicuous consumption by limiting the kinds of things associated with the Bar or Bat Mitzvah that could take place in the synagogue. We also tried to balance the party with community service requirements. I remember one time that a family's plans somehow slipped through. I arrived on Sunday morning to teach religious school to find that the synagogue had been turned into a Dungeons and Dragons set for a post–Bar Mitzvah fête—compliments of a New York set designer whom the family had hired just for this occasion.

Weddings

Depending on where you are in the evolution of your relationship, the wedding often looms large for couples. Weddings are relatively short ceremonies but they contain a few crucial items.

These rituals may be simple, but planning them properly may still be complicated, especially for interfaith couples. For a more extensive discussion of the issues relevant to interfaith weddings, see *Making a Successful Jewish Interfaith Marriage: The Jewish Outreach Institute Guide to Opportunities, Challenges and Resources* (Jewish Lights Publishing).

What the ceremony looks like will depend on the decisions you make as a couple, together with your officiant. In most cases, this will take a great deal of negotiating and compromise. Decide together what things are most important and what are issues of personal preference rather than principle. Since this book is an introduction to the Jewish faith and community, the description below follows a traditional Jewish pattern with the understanding that you may choose—as others have—to adopt and adapt various elements to reflect how you and your partner feel about your wedding.

The wedding ceremony is called *kiddushin,* from the Hebrew word for holy, but its root means "separate" or "consecrated." Thus, the wedding is holy because the individuals are separated out and consecrated to one another. The elements comprising the ceremony support this notion. While many of the rituals associated with a wedding ceremony have their origins in folk religion and therefore were linked to various superstitions, the Rabbis raised these rituals to greater spiritual heights and made them sacred as a result. Most Jewish wedding ceremonies do have elements in common, but community customs often make them distinct.

The *chuppah* or bridal canopy serves as a central focus for the ceremony. It represents the bridal chamber or the groom's tent. This is the ancient equivalent of the couple's bedroom on the one hand, and the home on the other. Sometimes, a *tallit* (prayer shawl) is used as a *chuppah*. Often it is more stylized and is made from silk and flowers.

The first person to go under the *chuppah* at a wedding ceremony will be the officiant, the rabbi or cantor. Older relatives like grandparents may lead the processional and be seated in the congregation but they do not stand under the *chuppah*. Like most weddings, the processional will usually include ushers and bridal attendants. In most cases, the bride and groom are accompanied separately by their parents—when they are able to do so—with the groom first and then the bride. The parents then take their place on the periphery of the *chuppah,* leaving room for the couple to stand under the *chuppah* itself with the officiant. The bride stands to the right of the groom. Others in the family—like brothers and sisters—may surround the perimeter of the *chuppah,* provided that they are part of the wedding party. Sometimes candles are used during the processional as a reminder that the wedding is a ceremony of joy and light or as a memorial to those family members no longer with us. In some ceremonies, the bride circles the groom. This is an elaborate circuit with layers of meaning, some of which hearken back to the time when brides were chattel, sold from fathers to husbands. Thus, the circuit symbolically emphasized a change in ownership, or a movement from the bride's father's home to her husband's. I explain it as a way of indicating the space that two individuals have made to become a couple and deem it as consecrated for the sacred purpose of marriage.

Following a formulaic blessing of welcome by the officiant, the ceremony continues in two sections. The first section, which begins with a blessing over wine, is actually the betrothal ceremony that at one time was separate and took place prior to the wedding. A second blessing is then recited, which affirms the institution of marriage. Oftentimes the rabbi or cantor separates this part of the ceremony from what follows with a mini-sermon.

The officiant may next call forward witnesses, as the groom places the ring on the bride's right index finger. The witnesses are there to confirm that the groom owns the ring. The index finger is used so that everyone can see it. (Since this is a legal ceremony, the ring is the article of value used to confirm the legal transaction.) The groom makes a formulaic statement that affirms the legal transaction (and perhaps raises it to a sacred level). In a double-ring ceremony, the bride places a ring on the finger of the groom. The bride generally makes a statement from the Song of Songs as a way of affirming the ring that she is giving to her husband. Some couples use this opportunity to share any personal words or to read poetry that expresses their love for each other.

Next, the *ketubah* (wedding contract) is read aloud, either entirely or in part, by either the officiant or by someone the couple wants to honor. There is a traditional text for the *ketubah*, but many couples use versions that reflect more modern sensibilities than does the language of the traditional *ketubah*.

The traditional seven wedding blessings are then read or chanted. Often couples invite friends or family members to recite individual blessings. These focus on the blessings for the couple and their future children, Jerusalem and Israel, and the continuity of the Jewish community. A second glass of wine is then shared by the couple. Following the blessings, a glass is broken, and the recessional begins. Why break the glass? A variety of explanations have been advanced, from taking time to pause in remembrance of the destruction of the ancient Temple in Jerusalem, to using it as a reminder of the fragility of life and of marriage. It has become so much a part of the Jewish wedding ceremony that its particular meanings have been transcended and it has become more ceremonial than symbolic.

Funerals and Mourning Practices

Recognizing that death is not a time for extensive ritual, Jewish funerals themselves are rather simple, with little in the way of pre-scribed liturgy. However, the customs associated with death and mourning are much more complicated. While many books explain these rituals, it is often better to seek the advice of a supportive and understanding rabbi, cantor, or other professional serving the Jewish community who can guide you through these mourning rit-uals and help ease the burden of making such decisions. Like so many other aspects of the Jewish religion, some of these mourning rituals are specified by Jewish law. However, many of these practices are guided by custom. Oftentimes, the customs eclipse the funeral and mourning practices and even appear more important. For a more in-depth look at the issues facing an interfaith couple when it comes to funerals, as well as the various Jewish communal or syn-agogue policies regarding burial in a Jewish cemetery, consult *Making a Successful Jewish Interfaith Marriage* (Jewish Lights Publishing). Many synagogues have policies that place restrictions on who may be buried in the synagogue cemetery. Communal organizations may be a little more flexible in this regard.

The process of mourning is divided into two segments. The first immediately follows the news that someone has died. The second phase begins with the interment of the deceased. While the Sabbath and holidays impact the timing of burial and mourning, Jews try to bury the deceased within twenty-fours of death. This places a great burden on family members who have to make arrangements, but it also forces the community to respond quickly to provide support for those who have lost a loved one. In a traditional community, the *chevra kaddisha* (literally, "holy society," a group of designated community members) assists with many of the arrangements, pre-pares the body, and stands guard over it until the funeral.

Before the funeral begins, members of the immediate family will be asked to either tear their clothing in a prescribed way or, more commonly, wear a torn black ribbon that indicates their status as a mourner. This ribbon is cut just before the funeral begins. The funeral has no fixed liturgy. It usually includes the recitation of psalms (frequently Psalms 23 and 127). Often Proverbs 31 is read during a funeral for a woman. In addition, a eulogy is offered. Unless there is a family member who wants to give the eulogy, the rabbi will do so. Even for people the rabbi or cantor knows well, he or she will prepare a eulogy after an in-depth discussion with members of the family of the deceased. At the end of the funeral, if it is not graveside, the prayer called *El Maleh Rachamim* ("God, Full of Compassion") is recited. Additional psalms may be recited at the grave, followed by a recitation of the *kaddish* memorial prayer. When the funeral does not take place in a funeral home or synagogue, these prayers are all said at the graveside.

Following the funeral, the family returns home to receive friends who want to express their sympathy. This is often referred to as a *shiva* call, a reference to *shiva* (meaning "seven"), the first seven days of mourning, which are the most intense. It is customary for friends to prepare the first meal for mourners. It is also customary for visitors to wait until mourners have spoken before addressing them, but this practice is rarely followed. Mourners will usually sit on stools or low seats to indicate their status as mourners, and a seven-day candle will be lit. Mirrors are covered as well. Why? Because it forces mourners not to focus on indulging themselves (no shaving, haircutting, or sexual relations, for example). Another explanation for this practice is that since human beings are created in the image of God, this reflection of God is somewhat diminished when one dies. Traditionally, *kaddish* is recited by the mourner three times a day as part of the regular pattern of fixed daily worship. This pattern continues throughout the first year of mourning.

Following the seven days of mourning, mourners take a walk around the block to symbolize their entrance into a new stage of mourning. This is called "getting up from *shiva.*" This stage, known as *sheloshim* (meaning "thirty"), refers to the first thirty days of mourning. During this stage, mourners return to much of their daily routine, including work, although public entertainment is avoided (as it is for the first twelve months).

Following the first thirty days, the mourner's routine returns to normal, as much as possible. Mourners follow this pattern for the rest of the first year (usually eleven months) until they observe the anniversary of the date of the loved one's death, called *yahrzeit.* At this time, memorial *kaddish* is once again recited, and mourners light memorial candles in their homes.

JEWISH INFLUENCE ON MUSIC, ART, AND LITERATURE

Some people assert that music, art, and literature are what shapes Jewish culture. And they do indeed contribute to Jewish "civilization," as conceptualized by Rabbi Mordechai Kaplan. Yet there are also those who say there is little that can be considered indigenous Jewish music, art, or literature. Perhaps micrography—the making of graphic art pictures through groups of small lettered words—is the only indigenous Jewish art form. Everything else is foreign in origin. Jewish communities have absorbed and adapted art forms from the surrounding cultures where Jews have lived throughout their historical dispersion.

Most talmudic Rabbis argued that human forms expressed in graphic art are prohibited as a classic Jewish art form, but we have plenty of examples in which human forms do, indeed, appear in Jewish artwork. The Jewish Theological Seminary, the

Conservative movement's rabbinical school in New York, is sensitive to this controversy. In its courtyard are numerous life-size statues. Considering the size of the bodies, however, the heads were intentionally made disproportionately small in order to avoid transgressing this law. There are also countless examples of illuminated manuscripts, such as medieval Italian *Haggadot*, illustrating the Passover narrative in graphic detail, that include human forms.

While literary styles are also adapted from surrounding culture, they are written in various languages, including Hebrew and the folk languages of the Jewish people, such as Yiddish and Ladino (a folk language of Sephardi Jews with Spanish roots). Prize-winning novelists such as Saul Bellow, Isaac Bashevis Singer, and Philip Roth have used literature to reflect their own interpretations of Jewish culture, and their Jewish writing has contributed to Western literature and become fully part of it as well.

Jewish culture has also entered the musical mainstream. Klezmer music is "in," for example. The word *klezmer* literally means "vessels of song." *Klezmer* tunes are so named because they were considered agents of musical exchange between the Jewish and secular world of Eastern Europe. They were played at weddings and during Purim and Simchat Torah celebrations. Today the *klezmer* style is noted for its trademark mix of strings and clarinet.

The greatest concentration of Nobel laureates, particularly in literature, are Jews. Members of the Jewish community also participate in much of the art community and support it. Thus, you will find Jewish influences in fine art, the decorative arts, stand-up comedy, and film. In turn, these fields have influenced Jewish culture. Some people claim that Jews made Hollywood a cultural force and continue to exert influence on it, even if the majority of actors and actresses are not Jewish (although many you'd never think were Jewish actually are). Certainly the major film studios were founded by Jews. Even the first films made by American Jews were based on the penny arcade minimovies made famous in New York's Lower East Side. Many famous film stars were Jews who "Americanized" their names. A certain style of humor is seen as distinctly Jewish: Think of the Woody Allen, Jackie Mason, Jerry Seinfeld continuum. Other elements of popular culture have also sprung from Jewish roots to become part of mainstream culture, such as chicken soup, matzah balls, and yiddishisms (like *oy vay*, "oh, my," and *schlemiel*, "poor soul who is out of luck").

CUSTOMS: POWERFUL AND PARTICULAR

As far as I am concerned, what gives Judaism and Jewish culture its distinctive flavor are the customs of its various communities. Customs are practices that have become part of the routine of a particular community. They are not necessarily governed by law. Sometimes, a custom is a community's individual interpretation of a particular law. Many people see Judaism and Jewish culture through the prism of Hollywood moviemaking. Some films may reflect real Jewish culture but most offer stereotyped and overstated images. Most people can't tell the difference between customs and Jewish law. Even for those who consider Jewish law to be binding, confusion between custom and law runs rampant. My late teacher Rabbi Jakob J. Petuchowski used to say—in reference to customs—that one generation's innovation is the next generation's sacred tradition. Thus, customs become more powerful than Jewish law in many respects because they get embedded in the signature identity of particular communities.

In my family we have many Jewish customs. Some are borrowed, others are adapted; still others we have fashioned on our own. For example, when we say a blessing over bread before we

eat (often referred to as "making *motzi*," a reference to the blessing that names God as the One who brings forth, *motzi*, the bread
from the earth) in my home, everyone who is gathered places a
hand on the bread, and if you can't reach, you place a hand on the
shoulder of the person who can reach. This way we truly all break
bread together. In one friend's home it is customary to tear the
bread by hand and then throw individual pieces to those gathered
around the table. In my editor's family, they light oil lamps on
Shabbat rather than candles, because they have spent time in an
artists' colony where there was no electricity and they eventually
began to enjoy the ambience of oil light. Because customs offer
inherent opportunities for creativity—and the addition of personal touches—they also give interfaith families a chance to make
their own contribution to the Jewish community in special ways.
Don't be afraid to be creative and develop your own family customs as your explore Judaism and the Jewish community.

NEXT STEPS

As someone new to the Jewish community, which aspects of
Jewish culture do you identify with? Think of Jewish works of art,
literature, music, film, and stand-up comedy that you've related
to. You can even get a Jewish cookbook and try out recipes. Just
let me know which ones you like—and I'll be right over.

4

Community: The Bonds that Bring People Together

There are many aspects to community. In a psychological sense, community can provide a sense of well-being, the assurance that one belongs to a group, an extended family of sorts. The religious concept of community is built around a set of requirements or religious obligations. In Judaism this refers to prayers that can only be said with a *minyan* of ten adults, the minimum requirement for community. Community can also refer to a geographical area or neighborhood, a place where people live harmoniously in a circumscribed physical space. In some cases these concepts overlap. We will look at all three as they relate to Judaism.

THE SIGNIFICANCE OF COMMUNITY

Community is one of the most powerful aspects of Judaism and the most difficult to explain. Usually, it is also the most challenging for Christians to understand and to navigate.

Thinkers such as Mordechai Kaplan have suggested that the Jewish community (the Jewish people, or the folk, as he liked to refer to it) is the most significant part of Jewish civilization, far more so than the Jewish religion, for without the Jewish community there can be no Jewish religion. The community is what provides the context for Jewish religion, and it is within the Jewish community that the ideas articulated in the religion take concrete form. This is significant because, as we've discussed, in Judaism action and behavior outweigh theory. For example, loving a neighbor as oneself—as instructed in the Torah—is of paramount importance in Jewish religion. This is done in various ways, particularly through acts of loving-kindness (*chesed* in Hebrew).

The Torah is quite specific about the prescribed acts of loving-kindness, such as "accompanying the dead to the grave," which describes the responsibility to provide a proper funeral in quite graphic terms. Ritual burial may be the only act of loving-kindness that is essentially pure and not motivated by anything else, since this act can never be repaid. It is thus referred to as *chesed shel emet* (literally, "true loving-kindness").

The traditional rituals of Jewish burial and mourning require the framework of community. In a traditional context, as soon as someone dies, members of the community spring into action. The body of the deceased is not left alone until it is interred. Out of respect for the individual, a group of community members, usually called the *chevre kaddisha* (literally, "holy society"), maintain a vigil over the body. They wash it in a prescribed way and say psalms during this time of "guarding." Following the funeral, community members prepare food for the mourners so that they do not have to worry about their own personal needs during this time. Rather than sending flowers, which is generally not the practice among Jews, people usually send food platters and fruit baskets as a way of expressing sympathy and fulfilling this obligation. People then assemble at the home of the mourners so that the *kaddish* memorial prayer may be said—and so that the mourners do not have to leave home for prayers during the first seven days (except for Shabbat). All of this ensures that people are not mourning alone and that the burden of grief is shared by others.

Thus, the community is an important force in the life of individuals and families, especially during life-cycle transitions. Often until you experience such a profound level of community interaction, you may not fully understand the importance of community life. This goes beyond specific ritual requirements and life-cycle events. For example, Donna, a close family friend of ours, required a liver transplant. After many years of struggling with a degenerative disease, her own liver was no longer able to support her. Unfortunately, Donna's insurance company refused to pay for the necessary surgery. In turn, the hospital was unwilling to perform the surgery unless she was able to pay for the surgery herself. Refusing to accept such a decision, my wife, Sheryl, went to work to raise the necessary funds. With the help of some friends, she mobilized a national campaign overnight. We used the Jewish community as a network, locally and nationally, and raised the required funds within two weeks. That's the power of community.

Just as the community can be large and powerful and a force for good, it can also be forbidding and difficult to enter. People seem to defer to some abstract notion of "Jewish community" despite their seeming lack of interest in religion or synagogue life. From the perspective of someone entering the Jewish community with a Christian background, it makes no sense: If it's so important to you, why not be actively Jewish? But to members of your Jewish family, there's no contradiction. What they may not understand is why you don't understand! They may even go as far as to say—infuriatingly—that you can *never* understand, and that is the problem. For me that attitude is at the heart of the problem. Family members may not be able to explain something that they feel deep in their gut. Granted, it may not lend itself to logical explanation, but we owe it to people like you who are joining our community, by marriage or any other way, to reach out and welcome you into our community. The first step is to convey to you what may be our idiosyncratic vision of community.

Historically, Jews had no choice about belonging to the Jewish community. If you were Jewish, you were in it. For one thing, Orthodox religion imposed community (or, more precisely, neighborhood) on the Jews, since Orthodox Jews had to live within walking distance of the synagogue: Traditional Jewish practice prohibits driving on Shabbat and holidays. Such practices preserve the sanctity of the Sabbath and holidays, and the community becomes a private realm set apart from the outside world. For one day a week the world of commerce is held at bay, because carrying money on Shabbat is anathema to traditional Jews. Since, historically, the Jewish community's religious authority also served as the local governing body, individuals had to turn to the community's appointed leadership for all civil matters, everything from resolving business disputes to officiating at life-cycle ceremonies such as weddings.

During certain periods Jews were forced by external authorities to live in specific areas (ghettos). Sometimes these boundaries were made with walls or natural borders like hills or rivers. This forced the segregation of the Jewish community and prevented interaction between Jews and non-Jews. The Pale of Settlement in Europe is a prime example. Established by Czar Elizabeth II in 1791 as a territory where Russian Jews could live, it was created under pressure to rid Moscow of competition from

Jewish business and Jews' "evil" influence on the Russian masses. The Pale of Settlement included the territory of what is now Latvia, Lithuania, Ukraine, and Belorussia. Even in the Pale, Jews were discriminated against by being forced to pay double taxes while being forbidden to lease land, run taverns, or receive higher education.

More subtle means were used to enforce segregation as well, such as designated areas where Jews weren't welcome—even if this policy was never expressly articulated. This occurred in many places as recently as a generation ago. I remember from my own childhood those neighborhoods where Jews didn't live and were not encouraged to move to. You may be familiar with areas like these in your own community. Some institutions, such as synagogues and Jewish Community Centers, continue to face difficulties when trying to build or expand their facilities, because neighbors fear that more Jews will move into the area. My own teacher, Jacob Rader Marcus, told me of an occasion about one hundred years ago in which a Jewish man bought land to build a home in one of the first suburbs outside downtown Cincinnati. Since Cincinnati was a pioneer town, he was surprised at the obstacles he encountered. He eventually abandoned his dream of building a home in that particular neighborhood—and did so in a more distant suburb. Instead, he deeded the area to the Jewish community as a cemetery, so that even paupers could be buried there!

Whether the community was developed from within or its boundaries were imposed by outside authorities, individual Jews had limited opportunities to live beyond the bounds of the Jewish community. Thus all were subject to its rules and its ways. This promoted a sense of group self-sufficiency that was built into the community structures for daily living.

This de facto segregation occurred even when the creation of the Jewish community was largely voluntary. In the United States, for example, as small groups of Jews moved to new cities, they first built cemeteries, then schools, then synagogues. Along the way came various charitable organizations to support those who needed assistance, especially those who lived far from their extended families and lacked traditional networks of support. Some community structures, such as Jewish hospitals (with names such as Mount Sinai in New York and Cedars of Lebanon in Los Angeles), were built by the Jewish community, in part because Jewish doctors were barred from internships or medical residencies in other generally church- and city-sponsored facilities. These facilities were also built for the sake of itinerant Jews, generally peddlers, who found themselves in cities far from home and unable to get health care when they became sick. Clearly, they were built for the benefit of the local Jewish community as well. Since Jewish patients and physicians are now welcome anywhere, many of these hospitals have been sold, with the proceeds placed into endowment funds to benefit the community. These funds have been used for projects in Jewish and secular communities. Such is the case with the Rose Community Foundation in Denver and the Jewish Heritage Foundation of Kansas City, Missouri, for example.

COMMUNITY IN LITURGY AND SACRED TEXTS

The notion of community rarely appears in the fixed liturgy. But while community may not affect *what* we pray, it certainly determines *how* we pray. For example, although you can pray by yourself, certain key prayers cannot be said unless there is a prayer quorum (a *minyan*). These prayers include the call to worship (*barkhu*) toward the beginning of the service; the sanctification (*k'dushah*) in the core of the service, toward the beginning of the *amidah;* and the mourner's *kaddish.* While the *kaddish* is general-ly known as the memorial prayer and comes at the end of the ser-vice, it also is used in various forms to mark the transition between sections or subsections of the service (similar to what musicians sometimes refer to as a half-stop or a full-stop). The public reading of Torah also requires a *minyan.* Some of these requirements reflect a certain inherent logic in the way formal liturgy functions. If you are praying by yourself or with one or two people, for example, a call to worship in the form of the *barkhu* prayer is unnecessary. The Reform movement has far more relaxed requirements for prayer, and most Reform rabbis do not require a *minyan* for the recitation of select communal prayers that otherwise would not be permitted to be said.

In a traditional community, the *minyan* must be made up of ten men. More liberal communities allow women to be counted among the ten. This is the case in most Conservative synagogues. The Reform movement accords women equal access and equal religious status.

There are specific prayers said on behalf of the community— and its leaders—as part of the standard worship service. For example, prayer service leaders offer healing prayers (often referred to as *mi sheberakh* prayers) for people in the community. Some congregations publicly share "blessings of the week" as a way of getting to know one another and thus building communi-ty. In my view, these prayers were added to the liturgy because of a belief in their efficacy, but I also think that they were included as a way of emphasizing the importance of community and com-munal leadership as a Jewish value.

The Jewish conception of community (and the *minyan* requirement) emerges from sacred text. Here we look to the biblical episode of the forward scouts—often translated as "spies"—sent ahead to evaluate whether Canaan was suitable for the Jewish people to inhabit, or the episode in which Abraham argues on behalf of the possible ten righteous people in Sodom and Gomorrah. In the first instance, Moses took the advice of Caleb and Joshua, two of the scouts—who said that the land flowed with milk and honey—instead of listening to the ten other scouts who said that the Land of Israel was uninhabitable and the people who lived there appeared to them as giants. For the Rabbis this defined the parameters for community: a minimum of ten. From the second passage, the Rabbis said that the idea that God would not destroy the cities if there were at least ten righteous people there confirms that ten is the minimum required for a place to be called a community.

Community itself is a powerful theme in the Bible. Much of the Book of Leviticus is built around the Temple cult. The efficacy of the Temple sacrifices determined the well-being of the community. Many of the sacrifices were offered on behalf of the community, rather than for the benefit by individuals. Nevertheless, the careful preparation of the sacrifices of individuals affected the welfare of the community as well. The community that grew up around the Temple and its practices may exemplify the development of the Jewish people, with the later liturgical system built as a replacement for the sacrificial system. While the concept and format of the synagogue predated the destruction of the Temple, once the Temple was destroyed synagogues became the primary model for community.

The commandments of the Torah emphasize the interests of the community. At the holiest time of the year (Yom Kippur), the holiest person (the high priest) enters the holiest place (the Holy of Holies, the innermost sanctum of the ancient Temple) in order to pray for the well-being of the community, after he prays for the well-being of himself and his family. And much of later rabbinic discussion is focused on what needs to be done to protect the sanctity and survival of the community.

An exclusiveness has been built into the Jewish religion. At certain times this was protective. Members of the Jewish community did and do fear outsiders, making the assumption that outsiders may threaten the health and stability of their community. In the early years of the Common Era, this may have been true quite literally. There were people, like the Gnostics, who tried to infiltrate the community by sneaking into the synagogue and changing the sacred writings, inserting different messages. Some religious rituals were designed to expose such attempts and to make sure this didn't happen. Unfortunately, exclusionary attitudes are still found in many synagogues and community organizations. One prime example is the practice of not allowing non-Jews affiliated with those institutions to hold board member positions.

I would argue, however, that the number of active and participating non-Jews in an increasing number of synagogues and in the general Jewish community demonstrates that outsiders can strengthen and enhance the Jewish community. This is changing attitudes across the board: Many synagogues and community organizations are striving to welcome and encourage those who come from outside the Jewish community to cast their lot with its members.

NAVIGATING THE STRUCTURES OF JEWISH COMMUNITY

The Jewish community structure looks complicated to the outsider. There seem to be so many moving parts: organizations, institutions, charities, and the like. To make matters worse, people often use multiple terms to refer to the same institution (synagogue, temple, or *shul*) or refer to these organizations and institutions in familiar shorthand (the Union, referring to the Reform movement or its congregational body, the Union for Reform Judaism, formerly known as the Union of American Hebrew Congregations, for example).

However, there is a clear overall structure, and once you learn a few key terms you can find your way around fairly easily. Most communities have a variety of synagogues, usually reflecting the ideology of the Reform, Conservative, Orthodox, or Reconstructionist movements. (The Reform movement is the largest in the United States, with the Conservative movement just behind. The Reconstructionist movement is the smallest but growing rapidly. See pp. 116–120 for more complete descriptions of the major movements in Judaism.) Some synagogues will identify in terms unrelated to the national movements. They may be part of smaller national movements, like Renewal, or simply refer to themselves by style, such as traditional. (This can mean Conservative-like, but not accepting women as equal in ritual, or Orthodox-like, but allowing mixed or family seating, which disqualifies it from the Union of Orthodox synagogues, referred to as the OU.) Knowing the differences between the movements will help you make a choice with regard to your own synagogue affiliation. However, the "feel" of individual synagogues sets them apart from one another more significantly than do their ideologies, as I mentioned earlier.

In addition to synagogues, many areas have a Jewish Federation, a kind of umbrella organization for Jewish community functions. These may have different names such as the United Jewish Appeal or the Council of Jewish Philanthropies. These Federations generally serve areas beyond the geographic limitations of specific metropolitan areas. For example, the UJA/Federation of New York, as it is called there, includes the five boroughs of New York City, Westchester County, and Long Island. Local Federations, in turn, belong to the United Jewish Communities, the national organization of local Federations (created by a recent merger of several national organizations charged with similar responsibilities, including the United Jewish Appeal, the United Israel Appeal, and the Council of Jewish Federations). This represents the so-called nonsynagogue, or secular, community and incorporates most Jewish social service organizations in the community. This national body has various partners that oversee the local community partners. For example, JESNA (Jewish Educational Services of North America) oversees the work of local Jewish educational organizations, generally known as "bureaus of Jewish education."

The Federation also serves as a voice for the local Jewish community. Its chief responsibility is to raise funds for distribution to local communal agencies (through a local allocations committee), to Israel (through the Jewish Agency), and to Jewish communities around the world (through the Joint Distribution Committee). Furthermore, depending on the size of the community, there are many local and national organizations that may address a certain topic or ideology. These include organizations such as Mazon, A Jewish Response to Hunger; Americans for Peace Now; and the Shalom Center. For most people the organized Jewish community is a veritable alphabet soup, since people refer to most of these organizations by their acronyms or by truncated forms of their names. All it takes is practice and familiarity to get a sense of the resources and services they provide. Here is a list of some of the more common ones you might encounter in your local community:

BJE: Bureau or Board of Jewish Education; coordinates educational efforts in the community

JCC: Jewish Community Center; cultural and recreational facility, usually with health club, nursery school, summer camp, and cultural events

JCRC: Jewish Community Relations Council; interacts with
       the secular community, especially in explaining the
       Jewish community to the larger community

JFS: Jewish Family Services; a social welfare agency (some-
       times called JFCS, Jewish Family and Children's
       Services) that provides therapy and counseling ser-
       vices, as well as life education programs

JVS: Jewish Vocational Services; provides career counseling
       and job placement

MANIFESTATIONS OF JEWISH COMMUNITY

What most people find remarkable about the Jewish community
is that even with all its internal disagreements Jewish communities look out for their members and members of Jewish communities throughout the world. In dire circumstances, spontaneous
fund-raising campaigns and emergency programs are launched,
but most of what is accomplished in a Jewish community occurs
through its organized structure. The deep sense of responsibility
for one another stems from a collection of specific *mitzvot* that
focus on this talmudic instruction: "All of Israel is responsible for
one another." This notion undergirds the commitment Jews feel
toward each other, and it is what motivates Jews to support local
institutions and even respond to anonymous requests to help fellow Jews in their community.

The commitment to community also shows itself in rallies
for Israel, as well as for imprisoned Jews and persecuted Jewish
communities throughout the world. Even as a child I remember
being amazed at how many people came together to raise money
for Israel during an emergency campaign in the course of the Six
Day War in 1967. As soon as the war broke out, mass rallies were
organized. In the small southern city where I was raised, we

joined together at the local Jewish Community Center. While we were worried about the survival of the State of Israel—this was perhaps the first time many were actually aware of its phoenixlike birth—we bore her burden with pride. I knew during those difficult days that I would spend extensive time living in Israel and make Israel a priority in my life. Even the study of Hebrew—normally a rather boring endeavor in religious school—took on new importance for me. I embraced the *yarmulke,* which was shunned in the Reform synagogue of my youth, as a symbol of Jewish identity and pride. At the time, this pride was more linked to Israel than to Jewish religion or religious practice. Rather than being overwhelmed by the crowd, I took comfort from the number of people who were there. It may have been only a few hundred, but I hadn't realized that there were that many Jews in our small community. In any event it was the first time that I had seen so many members of the Jewish community in one place. It was that memory that motivated me years later to organize large rallies exposing the plight of Soviet Jewry and to press for their release as part of the Student Struggle for Soviet Jewry.

This incalculable sense of community spills over into other areas of life and creates other opportunities. For example, connecting with Jews abroad adds a special dimension to travel. When we meet fellow Jews while traveling, we search out common experiences and people with whom we may be mutually acquainted. En route we are always on the lookout for synagogues, Jewish cultural institutions, kosher restaurants, and Jewish families traveling together.

Those who may be predisposed to anti-Semitism or rely on Jewish stereotypes use the special affinity that Jews have toward one another as a weapon against members of the Jewish community. They accuse Jewish people of controlling certain industries, such as banking and finance, through these relationships. Those who are neither supportive of the Jewish community nor critical of it may dismiss this "sixth sense" that some Jews have of picking out other Jews in a crowd as simply something related to a primal sense of survival. The reasoning goes something like this: we associate with others whose outlook is similar to ours as a way of protecting ourselves. There is strength in numbers, so we gravitate toward like-minded people when we meet them. But at various points in history finding other Jews was a matter of life and death. This was particularly true when Jews were fleeing their homes in Russia following a pogrom and seeking refuge among Jews in other communities. As they made their way to America, they may have been dependent on Jewish communities along the way.

Some Jewish communities are not as open or inclusive as they could be. As a result, a growing number of grass-roots organizations support alternative community structures and lifestyles such as *chavurot* (fellowship groups) or gay and lesbian synagogues. These organizations are often formed in communities whose institutions are not inclusive and welcoming. In other communities, the progressive secular culture nurtures the growth of such institutions. This is certainly the case in places like San Francisco where alternative institutions flourish, including the oldest interfaith program in the country, sponsored by the local Jewish Community Center.

Some institutions specify their inclusive stance in their stated policies, but you can't always rely on a paper trail. Nonetheless, when institutions are open to one subgroup, they are generally open to others. If you want to determine whether an institution is friendly and welcoming, start by making a telephone call. Consider how forthcoming the person is who answers, whether there is easy access to professional leadership, particularly the rabbi. Is the person on the telephone warm and welcoming, or cautious and standoffish? When you visit, pay attention to the same things. Do people say hello when you enter, or are they wary of strangers? When you attend services, do people extend themselves or stay in their own cliques? Do they go out of their way to say hello, ask if you are new in town, invite you to a community event, or even to their homes? If you are looking for a place that affirms the values that you consider important, take a look at the activities bulletin to determine the institution's program emphasis (youth, arts, education) and the opportunities it offers. When Jorge and Sharon moved to their new community, they were determined to find a synagogue that made them feel at home. Because they had moved to a large Jewish community, they had several synagogues to choose from. So each Friday and Saturday they tried out a different one. And they kept going for six months, until someone said hello, asked them whether they were new to the area, and invited them to their home for a meal—after they told them that they were an interfaith couple, raising Jewish children. One friend told me that he generally looks for a synagogue that caters to gay and lesbian Jews in the community. He is not gay, but he figures that if they are open and welcoming to those who are, then they would probably be welcoming to interfaith couples too. Unfortunately, however, this is not always the case.

THE "WHO IS A JEW" CONTROVERSY

Every so often, the ugly monster of "Who is a Jew?" rears its head. I call this question ugly, because it often casts doubt on people's religious identity, particularly converts to Judaism. This notion of "personal status," as it is technically called, concerns who is considered a Jew, how Judaism is passed from one generation to another, and how one can legitimately become a Jew. The question carries heavy emotional freight because the different movements, and even rabbis within a movement, disagree on these issues. The democratic nature of the United States allows for a variety of interpretations of Jewish law. This controversy is often fueled by decisions made by the chief rabbinate in Israel that relate to the Law of Return, an Israeli law that allows all Jews the right to citizenship in Israel. Recently, the law was amended once again, out of a fear that some foreign laborers brought to Israel during the first Intifada to replace Arab workers were converting to Judaism quickly just to enjoy the benefits of citizenship. To most American Jews, if you say you are Jewish, that's enough. They're not going to pry to find out which of your parents is Jewish or (if you are a man) whether you are circumcised—unless you are considering marriage and asking a rabbi to officiate at the wedding. Otherwise, your personal status may be irrelevant to most members of the community. Some people extend this question to various issues of Jewish law that require witnesses. For example, most consider it important that a person who signs the *ketubah,* a marriage document, be Jewish, as stipulated by Jewish law. Some rabbis use the issue of being accepted in Israel as a way of authenticating their own practice; one rabbi I know imposes certain requirements on weddings he performs, so that all the marriages will be accepted as valid in Israel. Technically, the question of who is Jewish is also relevant for honors in the synagogue, such as being called to the Torah or blowing the *shofar* during Rosh Hashanah and Yom Kippur.

Personally, I have a rather liberal perspective on this subject. I believe that the Jewish community should make it easier for willing individuals to cast their lot with the Jewish people. From a traditional perspective, however, there are only two ways that a person can be considered Jewish: if one's mother is Jewish or if one converts to Judaism according to traditional Jewish law or *halakha,* which includes *brit milah* (ritual circumcision) for boys, and *tevilah* (ritual immersion in a *mikvah*) for girls and boys. The Reform and Reconstructionist movements have broadened the rules in two ways. First, they also consider as Jewish anyone whose father is Jewish and who has been raised and educated as a Jew, irrespective of the faith of the mother. Second, the standards for conversion are not as rigorous. Not all Reconstructionist and Reform rabbis require circumcision for adults males, for example. Most religious decisions in Israel are currently made by the chief rabbinate (one for Ashkenazi Jews and one for Sephardi Jews), and at this time liberal perspectives on this issue tend to be rejected out of hand. There is no "chief rabbi" in the United States; this is why the different denominations' rulings are so significant. At one time there were attempts to create a chief rabbinate in New York, to no avail. Some countries, such as the United Kingdom, maintain the office of chief rabbi, but the chief rabbi speaks more for the Orthodox community than for the others. In those communities that do have chief rabbis today, the office is more honorific than anything else.

CONCERN FOR OTHER COMMUNITIES

The Jewish feeling of obligation for one another is particularly acute in the case of endangered and persecuted Jewish communities. Thus, the *mitzvah* of "redeeming the captive" (*pidyon shevuim* in Hebrew) mobilizes the community. Maimonides considered the "redemption of the captive" to be the primary *mitzvah* of the individual, calling it a core obligation, above all else. For him this *mitzvah* encapsulated all of Jewish values. We are responsible to free our persecuted brethren, as we are required to free other persecuted peoples. The Jewish people, because of its own history, identifies profoundly with persecuted peoples, regardless of their background. This idea is echoed in the formal liturgy as well; God is acknowledged as the one who redeems the captive. Since we are obligated to mimic God's work, we have to follow the divine lead. Some argue that God's work is, in fact, accomplished by human hands.

In this generation we have seen entire Jewish communities rescued from the former Soviet Union and Ethiopia. In previous generations the liberation of Jews took place in Yemen, Syria, Iraq, and other countries, particularly following World War II. Many Jews from these countries went directly to Israel. Others, particularly from the former Soviet Union, settled throughout the United States. They were offered housing and given vocational guidance, training, and jobs. They were welcomed as synagogue members and their children attended Jewish day schools on scholarship.

SYNAGOGUE AS COMMUNITY BASE

Among the various institutions in the Jewish community, the synagogue, more than any other, embodies community values. In some respects the synagogue is a microcosm of the Jewish community. Since Jews no longer live primarily in Jewish neighborhoods, the synagogue is usually the primary vehicle for forming Jewish community. Thus, we often equate the synagogue community with the Jewish community.

The classic understanding of the synagogue is that it serves as a place for prayer, study, and assembly. In all three cases its major function is to build and nurture community. There are certain quorum (*minyan*) requirements for various parts of the formal worship service. These requirements force observant Jews to maintain the notion of a community. One prayer that requires a *minyan* is the *kaddish*, or memorial prayer, said by mourners three times a day during the first year following the death of a parent. Synagogue members may be called to participate in an early morning *minyan* to enable someone to say *kaddish*. People who may not otherwise attend the service take this on as a responsibility to their community.

It is ironic, therefore, that many Jews do not belong to a synagogue; estimates range from 40 to 60 percent nationally. Yet these same Jews may affirm the role of the synagogue as primary in the Jewish community; even if they don't go, they are usually glad that the synagogue is there. This may differ significantly from the relationship that your family has with the local church in their community. In many communities, the synagogue plays a public relations role of sorts and represents the Jewish community to the secular and the Christian community. Synagogues often sponsor events and support local organizations, such as soup kitchens, to maintain good relations with the general community (and to perform acts of *tikkun olam*), and members of the synagogue, as well as the rabbi, may take positions on community issues to make sure that the so-called "Jewish position" is represented.

No discussion of synagogues is complete without mentioning the practice of membership dues and fees for religious school education and tickets to attend worship services for the High Holidays. While some congregations are experimenting with alternative dues structures or no dues at all, the American Jewish community adapted from Europe the idea of a community tax for the support of Jewish institutions and tailored it to the voluntary organizational structure of the synagogue. The European practice has its roots in the biblical notion of community support for the Temple enterprise. By collecting dues, synagogues tried to avoid a fee-for-service arrangement with community members. Thus, members of synagogues were entitled to all the services provided. Some people may argue that dues were charged instead of following the practice of churches that "pass the collection plate" because traditionally Jews do not handle money on Shabbat (stemming from the requirement to refrain from commerce of any kind on the Sabbath). Decisions to charge for High Holiday tickets and religious school education are more than simply ways to generate sorely needed funds to support the synagogue. Rather, these choices have specific philosophical underpinnings. For example, when a synagogue charges families tuition for religious school, it is saying that the future of the institution and the education of its children are the responsibilities of individual parents rather than the responsibilities of the institution as a whole or its entire membership. The charge for High Holiday tickets is a reflection of operating in a free-market economy.

THE FOUR MAJOR MOVEMENTS IN AMERICAN JUDAISM

There are four main Jewish religious movements in the United States and Canada. However, individual synagogues vary a great deal in their style and approach, particularly when it comes to worship, even among synagogues of the same movement. No movement is "one size fits all."

Reform

With roots in Germany, the Reform movement is the largest and oldest synagogue movement in North America, having been established in the nineteenth century. What sets it apart from the other movements is its contention that Jewish law is not divine in origin— that is, that the Torah was not revealed to the Jewish people on Mount Sinai at a specific time. Rather, it was written by human beings with divine inspiration. Thus the rules and practices of Judaism may be modified based on human judgment. As a result, members of the Reform movement represent a wide diversity in practice. The primary focus of the movement is on its affirmation of personal autonomy. Such personal decision-making when it comes to ritual and practice often leads individuals to choose to forgo rituals and practices that do not reflect contemporary mores and values. On a national level, direction for the movement is equally divided between rabbis, congregations, and the movement's rabbinical training seminary, Hebrew Union College–Jewish Institute of Religion (HUC–JIR).

Reform ideology rejects the classic Jewish notions of resurrection of the body in the afterlife and the idea of a personal messiah. On the social front, the Reform movement was an early champion of women's equality in Judaism, ordaining the first woman in the United States as a rabbi (Sally Priesand) at Hebrew Union College–Jewish Institute of Religion. Taking its cue from the Hebrew prophets, the movement has always been a strong advocate of social justice and social action to make society better.

Conservative

The Conservative movement was developed as a reaction to early and often controversial decisions and practices of the Reform movement, primarily in the early years of the twentieth century. Therefore, it is the second oldest American Jewish religious movement. It traces its roots to the historical school of Judaism in Europe. This school of thought attempted to stem the tide of assimilation brought on by the Enlightenment by applying the tools of history to the study of traditional Judaism and its practices. It maintained a strong commitment to Jewish nationhood, the Land of Israel, and the Hebrew language. It sought to *conserve* Judaism in the modern context.

The Conservative movement is a seminary-led movement, with the Jewish Theological Seminary at the helm. The law committee of its rabbinical organization (the Standards and Laws

Committee of the Rabbinical Assembly) shapes the decisions for observance as it carefully walks the difficult path between tradition and modernity. Since it does not reject the binding nature of Jewish law but is also cognizant of the challenges of the contemporary world, it seeks to strike a feasible balance between the two. Unlike the Reform movement, it hesitates to draw sharp ideological lines between itself and the other movements.

Reconstructionist

This movement is the smallest and youngest, but it is growing quickly. While it might be considered to have grown out of the Conservative movement, it influences all the other movements as a result of the impact of the ideas of its founder, Rabbi Mordechai Kaplan. Its seminal synagogue institution, the Society for the Advancement of Judaism, was founded in New York City in 1922, but the Reconstructionist Federation was not founded until 1955. Kaplan sought to apply social science and Western democratic values to Judaism and *reconstruct* it in the process. He saw Judaism as an evolving civilization, not only a religion. The movement is socially progressive: Reconstructionist leaders were early champions of women's and gay rights within the Jewish community.

Borrowing from social theory, the Reconstructionist movement asserts that the decisions of the community take precedence over the decisions of the individual. Like the Reform movement, it rejects the traditional notion of the revelation of Torah at Mount Sinai. Reconstructionism also rejects the notion of a personal God who can intervene supernaturally in the world. Instead, it sees contemporary Judaism as the evolving result of the adaptation of Jewish religion and culture as it traveled through history from place to place. The movement does not see Jewish practices as the commandments of God. Rather, they are considered precious expressions of the past, part of the historical context in which they originated. While these Jewish traditions are treasured, it is the responsibility of each generation as a community—rather than as individuals—to evaluate such traditions and measure their value for the contemporary community. The Jewish people become the most important variable in such a reconstruction of Judaism. Reconstructionist Jews have always been advocates for the State of Israel, even as they have been strong advocates for America.

Orthodox

This is the modern designation for the part of the Jewish community that is most traditional and whose decisions are based strictly on Jewish law. The perspective of Orthodoxy is that this law was given to the Jewish people by God on Mount Sinai. The term *Orthodoxy* is borrowed from the Christian community and was used first by Reform Jews in the nineteenth century to refer to those who remained faithful to the practices and customs it was questioning. While there had been a range of practices in traditional Judaism up to the Middle Ages, Orthodoxy became quite fixed following the issuance of the first law codes during the medieval period. Nevertheless, there remains a great deal of diversity within the Orthodox community. From the outside it looks like there is little contemporary flexibility in practice among Orthodox Jews, but they too are struggling to react positively within their own parameters to various aspects of modernity, such as the rights of women. Orthodoxy as a movement might be said to represent a continuum of Orthodox groups that includes those far to the right, such as the so-called settlers' movement in Israel as well as various communities of Hasidim and those liberal Orthodox groups that refer to themselves as centrists.

Orthodoxy rejects the so-called progressive revelation, which is a tenet of Reform Judaism. It also denies most forms of historical criticism of sacred text. In the synagogue one of the most salient features is that men and women do not sit together in prayer.

Jewish Literacy Opens Doors

The goal of community extends beyond one's home turf and reaches into any Jewish community—or synagogue. When my wife and I were raising our own children, our goal was straightforward. We wanted to provide our sons with the kind of education and Jewish experiences that would permit them to feel comfortable and literate in any synagogue in the world, regardless of movement or the way worship might be conducted in that particular institution. We wanted them to be able to tap into many forms of Judaism and thus many communities. This required a high level of education and exposure to a multiplicity of experiences.

It is an important Jewish value to feel comfortable and welcomed in synagogues everywhere. The challenge is to appreciate the synagogue on its own terms, from the perspective of an insider, rather than judging it. That is what Jews expect from the Jewish community, and they will often seek out local synagogues when they travel. Many people will bring suggestions to their local synagogue based on their experiences elsewhere. Sometimes it is as simple as a melody for a certain prayer. Other times it is more complex, regarding customs and practices. People have a sense that this broadens their Judaism, and that bringing this experience home ultimately enriches their own community.

This raises the topic of Jewish cultural literacy. Jewish literacy is basic knowledge of the "stuff" of Jewish culture: dates, people, places, holidays, customs, and values. Many people feel unsure about their level of knowledge and thus hold themselves back. It is not easy to navigate the Jewish community—particularly the synagogue community—if you are not Jewishly literate. Keep in mind, however, that literacy evolves through the accumulation of Jewish experiences more than from information acquired from books. *Doing* creates *knowing*. Jewish literacy grows out of memories and shared experiences. Every time you reach out to a new Jewish group or partake in a ritual new to you, you are building shared knowledge and thus community.

ISRAEL'S ROLE IN AMERICAN JUDAISM

The modern State of Israel plays an indispensable role in the life of every American Jew. While the connection that most American Jews—particularly younger ones—have with Israel is not as visceral and immediate as it was, say, in the years following the Six Day War in 1967, the destiny of the American Jewish community is inextricably tied to the future of Israel. This is more than affirming the concrete notion of the Jewish people's self-determination, and it is more than the playing out of Jewish values against the backdrop of a difficult political reality. Israel is a centerpiece of Jewish communal living. Attitudes toward Israel often reflect attitudes toward the Jewish community. It becomes a barometer for the comfort and security that Jews feel in the world.

I know that the first thing that I read in the newspaper each day is news about Israel. Because of the time difference, I want to know what happened during the daytime hours in Israel while I was sleeping. My wife and I have traveled extensively in Israel. Most of our family vacations have centered on Israel. Whenever we have the opportunity, even if only for a short time, we go to Israel, sometimes just to walk the streets of Jerusalem and spend Shabbat there. We believe that Israel is the crossroads for Jewish communal life. When we are there, we feel connected to Jews past and present, here and everywhere.

For us and for many others throughout Jewish history, Jerusalem has served as the spiritual center of the Jewish people. The Rabbis say that Jerusalem is the place where heaven and earth meet. Heavenly Jerusalem *(Yerushalayim shel malah)* stands above earthy Jerusalem *(Yerushalayim shel matah)* as parallel worlds of sorts. The interface between Israel and the American Jewish community operates on several levels. There are sister-city programs, student-exchange programs, and adult-study programs where Americans and Israelis study together by long distance. Just about every Jewish community offers grants for young people to go to Israel on a variety of programs. There are intensive Hebrew language immersion programs called *ulpanim* (singular, *ulpan*). There was a time when working on a kibbutz in Israel was virtually a rite of passage for young American Jews. I spent one month on a kibbutz when I was sixteen years old. By putting me into direct contact with the soil, it nourished my roots and was thus a transformative experience. The dream of Israel's first prime minister, David Ben Gurion, was that every Jew would spend at least some time in Israel.

Perhaps now, more than ever, on a political level American Jews are feeling some ambivalence toward Israel as it takes its steps and missteps toward peace. The attitudes regarding Israel's everyday political actions and even religious decisions are often polarized, with feelings running high on all sides. Some newcomers to the Jewish community may find the tension between supporting Israel and sometimes disagreeing with Israel's policies to be confusing, as do many Jews. This difference of opinion is healthy. It fosters creative growth, even as it reveals uncomfortable and underlying fault lines within the Jewish community. As a reflection of this reality, there are a range of organizations that deal with Israel, from the American Israel Public Affairs Committee (a pro-Israel lobby or PAC [political action committee]) to Americans for Peace Now (a liberal, pro-peace group). Many American Jews go out of their way to express their politics regarding Israel—it's that central to them. To Jews the world over, Israel's existence is an insurance policy against another Holocaust, although most American Jews aren't considering immigration to Israel *(aliyah)*. And there is a tradition of *aliyah* throughout Jewish history (the same word, *aliyah,* is used for a Torah honor, literally "going up" to the Torah). Since Israel was founded as a result of the Holocaust and many survivors were among its founders, there is a strong emotional connection between Israel and the Holocaust. Most Jews believe that, had Israel existed in the 1930s, there would have been no Holocaust.

ZIONISM: BOTH POLITICAL AND SPIRITUAL

The focus on Israel is not new to the Jewish community. Even though the State of Israel emerged as a direct result of the Holocaust, the modern movement toward an independent Jewish state predates World War II. The struggle for Jewish self-government and independent rule began as soon as that autonomy was lost to the Romans in 70 C.E. Key components of the liturgy reflect this view. For example, each Passover seder concludes with the words *next year in Jerusalem.* Like so many other aspects of fixed rituals, oft-repeated important liturgical verses can become routine. However, one could argue that the entire seder experience is designed just for the sake of that one line and what it represents:

"We were slaves in Egypt; we remain slaves in dispersed lands. When we reach Jerusalem—let it be within the coming year—we will know true freedom: freedom of the body and of the soul." This is at once a political and a spiritual statement: May we all celebrate next year in Jerusalem; may we all celebrate next year with a Jerusalem state of mind. It is a messianic dream. One might say that Jerusalem and Israel serve as spiritual metaphors.

For some, Zionism is a secular movement that is solely about self-rule. For others, Zionism and the return to Israel are religious, part of God's plan for the world and the ushering in of the Messianic Era. For fundamentalist Christians, the Jewish return to Israel is a precursor to the Second Coming. But Zionism is a political movement that needs to be distinguished from the religious and emotional Jewish commitment to Israel. As a matter of fact, since some Zionists were interested only in self-government, irrespective of where such a government would be established, the Jewish people was offered Uganda and other places as possible sites for a Jewish state between 1903 and 1905. But these offers were rejected, since only Israel resonated with the Jewish journey through history.

Theodor Herzl is credited with jump-starting the modern Zionist movement. Herzl, an Austrian journalist, was an assimilated Jew. In 1894 he was sent to France to cover the trial of Alfred Dreyfus, who was accused of handing over military secrets to the Germans. Herzl concluded that the trumped-up treason charges were a mere pretext, and that Dreyfus was essentially on trial for being a Jew. Covering the trial transformed Herzl and set him on a path that eventually led to the movement to create a Jewish state.

American Jewish economic support of Israel is vital to its survival, as is the support of the American government. Jews support Israel in a variety of ways. There are common and traditional means, such as donating funds to the local Jewish Federation, a large portion of which goes directly to Israel. The Jewish Federation also collects for the Israel Emergency Fund, usually activated when Israel is experiencing a particular threat, like the Intifada or a war such as the Yom Kippur War of 1973. Israel Bonds are also sold by the Development Corporation for Israel, an organization created just for this purpose. Many synagogues sponsor events at which Israel Bonds are sold. It takes some getting used to (and I, for one, have never gotten used to it), but sales pitches for Israel Bonds are often made during Rosh Hashanah or Yom Kippur services in the synagogue. Funds are not collected at the time, since it would be contrary to traditional Jewish law to do so, but pledges are made. This is typically done through the use of cleverly designed, pre-folded cards that are handed out with prayer books and then collected following the pitch. The Jewish National Fund, well known for its reforestation project and the "blue boxes" used for collecting coins, is another major vehicle for support for Israel. These blue boxes are ubiquitous in Jewish religious schools. While the JNF has undergone some serious challenges over the last few years, it remains committed to building up Israel through the planting of trees and forests, harnessing solar energy, and investing in other development and environmental projects.

Another way to support Israel economically and emotionally is through travel. Often such travel takes place in the form of missions. These trips are sponsored by particular organizations like the Jewish Federation, which show you Israel from that organization's perspective. While this is not my preferred way to travel, the mission method does inspire people to give more money to Israel. However, the heavy-handed fund raising can also be alienating, intimidating, and off-putting, especially for those who are just finding their footing in the Jewish community. Creative individuals are developing innovative ways to tour Israel all the time, such as through outdoor adventure trips or extensive volunteer programs. The Palmers, an interfaith family, returned from such a trip with their children and told me about their experience: "We were thrilled. We told the guide to go easy on the archaeology and religious sites. We wanted to do 'family Israel' and he came through. As a result, there was no religious tension on the trip at all."

Psychologically, foreign visitors are extremely important to Israelis. At times during the Intifada, when fewer Americans were traveling to Israel, people there really felt abandoned. As a result, many people made a point of emphasizing the need to support Israel not in the abstract but by actually going there to show their care and commitment on a personal level. Mind you, that kind of support has nothing to do with agreeing or disagreeing with the policies of any Israeli government. People in Israel feel as if they are on the frontier and they are maintaining their presence on behalf of all Jews.

There are also nontraditional ways of supporting Israel that may better reflect your values. For example, the New Israel Fund was established as an alternative means of aiding organizations and institutions not generally supported by the Federation system (called the United Jewish Communities). It is also a way for those who don't support some of the policies of the government to provide humanitarian funds for Israel, while making sure that those funds do not go to support programs that may conflict with their beliefs. One divisive issue is the support of settlements on the other side of the Green Line, the pre-1967, Six Day War boundary that was established following the 1948 war of independence. This is not a simple matter—since there is a difference between housing developments that are built in security rings around Jerusalem and are more like suburbs, and isolated settlements in the midst of Arab communities, such as Hebron, and in the Gaza Strip. The most popular nontraditional approach to supporting Israel—especially considering that travel to Israel has diminished significantly since the start of the Intifada and post–September 11—is to buy Israeli products. This is generally referred to by the slogan, "Buy Israel." Websites like www.ShopIsrael.com have been developed so that people can access Israeli products more readily, and Israelis can show their wares to people outside of Israel. Think about purchasing Israeli products whenever you're shopping, whether you're looking for clothing or something for your home, especially ritual objects. Make a point of purchasing Israeli products in preparation for the celebration of holidays, when including something from Israel infuses the holiday with even greater meaning.

NEXT STEPS

Venture into the community. Attend a public Jewish communal gathering or an open board meeting of a Jewish communal agency whose work interests you. Volunteer if you are inclined to be of help to that agency or organization.

Summary of Major Jewish Holidays

Rosh Hashanah (New Year)
> Marks the beginning of the religious year; occurs in September/ October.

Yom Kippur (Day of Atonement)
> A day for introspection and vows for self-improvement; occurs ten days after Rosh Hashanah in September/October.

Sukkot (Festival of Booths)
> Celebrates the fall harvest and the wandering of the ancient Israelites in the desert; occurs in the fall.

**Shemini Atzeret and Simchat Torah
(Eighth Solemn Day of Assembly and Joyful
Celebration of the Torah)**
> Occur at the end of the Sukkot festival in the fall. Shemini Atzeret is noted for its prayer for rain at the beginning of Israel's rainy season, and Simchat Torah marks the end and new beginning of the cycle for the public reading of the Torah.

Hanukkah (Festival of Rededication)
Recollects the eight-day rededication of the ancient Temple in Jerusalem; occurs in late November/December.

Tu Bishevat (Jewish Arbor Day)
A celebration of Judaism and the environment; occurs in late January/early February.

Purim (Festival of Lots)
Celebrates the saving of the ancient Persian Jewish community; occurs in late winter.

Pesach (Passover)
Marks the deliverance from Egyptian slavery of the ancient Israelites and the beginning of their desert wanderings; occurs in early spring.

Yom Hashoah (Holocaust Memorial Day)
A modern commemoration of the Jews who perished during World War II; occurs in late spring.

Yom Ha'atzmaut (Israel Independence Day)
Celebration of Israel's independence; occurs one week after Yom Hashoah in late spring.

Shavuot (Festival of Weeks)
A spring harvest festival of the first fruits and the celebration of the giving of the Torah; occurs in late spring/early summer.

Tisha B'av (Ninth Day of Av)
Commemorates the destruction of the Temple in 586 B.C.E., as well as other painful moments in Jewish history; occurs in late summer.

Glossary

afikoman: A piece of matzah that is broken and hidden during the Passover seder. Children are invited to look for it and hold it for "ransom" from the seder leader.

aliyah: Literally, "going up"; the term used for both immigration to Israel and a Torah honor in the synagogue, when the individual ascends the *bimah.*

amidah: The "standing prayer"; the nineteen benedictions that constitute the core of the daily prayer service, which is recited three times a day by traditional Jews; also called the *shemonah esrei* (literally, "eighteen," for the original eighteen blessings it contained) or *hatefilla* (literally, "the prayer," since it is the core prayer in the fixed liturgy).

Aron haKodesh: The Holy Ark, a special cabinet for holding the Torah, generally located in the front of a synagogue's sanctuary.

Ashkenazi: Referring to Jews from countries descended from the Germanic kingdoms, meaning Eastern Europe and Russia, in general.

Bar/Bat Mitzvah: The ceremony that marks the religious coming of age for boys (Bar Mitzvah) and for girls (Bat Mitzvah, sometimes written as Bas Mitzvah) following which they become responsible for their actions under Jewish law and are called on to undertake religious and community obligations. Boys become Bar Mitzvah at thirteen years of age. Girls may celebrate their Bat Mitzvah at twelve, but most girls celebrate at age thirteen.

barkhu: The call to worship, toward the beginning of the worship service.

barukh haba: Welcome; literally, "you are blessed in your coming."

bikkurim: "First fruits" or "choice fruits" of the spring harvest, originally brought as offerings to the ancient Temple; associated with the holiday of Shavuot.

bimah: Raised platform in the center or front of the sanctuary where the Torah is read.

bris, brit milah: Ritual circumcision.

challah: Egg twist bread, used at Sabbath and holiday meals; generally in braided loaves for the Sabbath and round loaves for other occasions, such as the High Holidays.

charoset: Mixture of apples, cinnamon, nuts, and wine, symbolizing the mortar used by the Israelite slaves; part of the Passover seder.

chavurah (pl. *chavurot*): Fellowship group, usually formed around a common interest or life experience.

chesed shel emet: "True act of loving-kindness." Generally refers to the act of burial, since it can never be repaid. Also used in reference to "paupers' graves" in a Jewish cemetery.

chevre kaddisha: Burial society; a group of individuals who undertake the task of preparing a body for interment.

chevruta: Study partner in the traditional model of cooperative learning.

chutzpah clappei malah: Literally, "guts and gumption in the face of heaven," that is, God. This establishes a mind-set for prayer for some people as they confront God angrily in response to their displeasure over divine actions.

davenning: Yiddish word for the traditional mode of Jewish prayer that usually includes swaying back and forth, a motion referred to as *shuckling.*

devekus: "Soul attachment," akin to the modern Hebrew word for "glue" *(devek).*

Diaspora: The scattering of the Jewish community following its exile from the Land of Israel in 586 B.C.E.

dreidel: Yiddish for spinning top, *s'vivon* in Hebrew; a game that tells the "miracle" story of Hanukkah.

dvar Torah (pl. *divrei* Torah): Short explanation of a Torah reading.

Edot Hamizrach: Literally, "Eastern communities," referring to Jews who live in the East, primarily in Arab lands.

gemilut chasadim: Good deeds; "acts of loving-kindness."

ger: Literally, "stranger"; refers to converts to Judaism.

ger toshav: Resident alien; a biblical term for non-Jews who live among Jews.

Haggadah: Prayer book guide for the Passover seder that chronicles the story of the Israelites' experience of slavery in Egypt, their Exodus, and their journey in the desert.

Haftarah: Reading from the Prophets and Writings, following the public reading of the Torah.

Hakodesh Barukh Hu: A name for God, literally, "The Holy One, Blessed be He," often referred to as The Holy Blessed One or The Holy One of Blessing.

halakha: Jewish law.

hamantaschen: Triangular cookie served at Purim. It is a pun on the Yiddish word *man* (poppy) and *taschen* (pockets) and the name of the central villain in the Purim story: Haman. Called *oznei-Haman* (literally, "Haman's ears") in Hebrew.

Hasidism: Antiformalist movement of Jews that originated in Poland in the seventeenth century, led by the charismatic Baal Shem Tov. Contemporary adherents still wear the distinctive garb from the period, including fur-trimmed hats and long black coats. Most well known of the Hasidic communities are the Lubavitcher Hasidim (also known as Chabad).

hekhsher: Kosher license or imprimatur given by a rabbi or rabbinical body.

Jews by Choice: Politically correct term for converts to Judaism or proselytes.

Kabbalah: Jewish mysticism.

kaddish: Generally refers to the memorial prayer but also refers to the prayer that marks transitions between parts of the worship service.

kaddishel: This is a Yiddish expression (that comes from the Hebrew word *kaddish,* the memorial prayer for the dead). It implies that the individual, the *kaddishel,* will say *kaddish,* for his or her parent and thereby keep alive the parent's memory.

kashrut: System of Jewish kosher dietary laws.

kavannah: "Intention"; spontaneous prayer (as opposed to *keva,* "fixed prayer"); also refers to sacred texts used as mantras.

k'dushah: The sanctification, toward the beginning of the *amidah,* a prayer recited by the service leader (usually the cantor).

ketubah: Marriage certificate.

kibbutz: A farming collective in Israel based on a socialist ideological model.

kibud av va'em: "Honoring father and mother."

kiddush: Sanctification prayer said over wine for Sabbath, holidays, and at life-cycle events.

kippah: Skullcap, also known by the Yiddish *yarmulke.*

latkes: Potato pancakes, the primary food associated with Hanukkah because it is fried in oil.

l'shma: "For its own sake," usually referring to study.

maror: Bitter herbs, usually horseradish, used in the Passover seder.

matzah (pl. *matzot*): Flat unleavened bread, the central symbol of the holiday of Passover; made without leavening because it was hastily prepared and carried when the Israelites fled Egypt upon their deliverance from slavery (about 1250 B.C.E.).

melekh: "King," a traditional name for God.

melekh malkhei hamlakhim: "King of Kings," a traditional name for God.

menorah (pl. *menorot*): Also called *hanukkiyah;* specially designed candelabra for ritual use during Hanukkah. Adapted from the menorah in the ancient Temple of Jerusalem (which had seven candles, one for each day of creation), Hanukkah *menorot* have eight branches (symbolizing the eight days of the holiday of rededication) with a ninth candle—termed a server candle, or *shamash*—used to light the other eight.

Midrash: Refers to the parablelike sections of the Talmud and rabbinic literature containing biblical interpretations; sometimes referred to as legends.

mikvah: Ritual bath.

minyan: Quorum of ten, required for certain prayers.

mi sheberakh: Literally, "the One who blesses"; a reference to prayers that are said primarily to ask for the health and well-being of others.

Mishnah: The first written summary of Jewish law, compiled in the Land of Israel about the year 200 C.E. and therefore the first overall written evidence for the state of Jewish prayer in the early centuries.

mitzvah (pl. *mitzvot*): Commandments, refers to 613 sacred obligations incumbent on Jews, as directed by God. The term is often used more generally to refer to good works or good deeds.

m'kor chayyim: "Source of Life," an alternative name for God, used particularly by Jewish feminists.

mohel: The person who performs the ritual of circumcision, trained and certified for this purpose, or a physician trained by the Jewish community to combine the ritual elements and medical practice, often assisted by a local rabbi.

nusach: Music used to chant the liturgy.

oral law: According to tradition, this spoken law was given to Moses on Mount Sinai, along with the written law of the Torah, and then transmitted from teacher to student and from parent to child, orally from one generation to the next, until it was written down as the Talmud many years later.

pareve: Neutral, containing neither meat nor milk; can be used idiomatically as a synonym for "bland" in a variety of contexts.

Passover (*Pesach* in Hebrew)**:** Springtime festival that celebrates the deliverance of the ancient Israelites from Egyptian slavery. The Hebrew word *pesach* refers to the sacrificial offering of a lamb associated with the festival.

Pirkei Avot: Meaning "Ethics of the Ancestors," an interesting collection of rabbinic aphorisms in the Mishnah that offer insight and wisdom for daily living.

pidyon shevuim: Redeeming or rescuing the captive.

pushke: Yiddish for *tzedakah* (charity) container, or charity collection box.

Rosh Hashanah: Jewish New Year; occurs in the fall.

seder: The table ceremony held on Passover that celebrates the holiday and retells the Exodus using the Haggadah. (In Hebrew, *seder* means "order.")

Sephardi: Referring to Jews who live in communities originally descended from Spain.

Shavuot: Late spring/early summer harvest festival that celebrates the giving of the Torah on Mount Sinai.

Shekhinah: The indwelling presence of God; usually used to refer to God's feminine attributes.

Shema Yisrael: Often called the watchword of the Jewish faith, this is the closest thing to a Jewish creed; it proclaims the unity of one God.

shofar: A ram's horn used for ritual purposes, primarily on Rosh Hashanah and Yom Kippur.

shul: Yiddish for synagogue.

Simchat Torah: Fall holiday immediately following Sukkot that is a celebration of Torah and marks the time when weekly Torah reading is concluded for the year and begun once again.

sukkah (pl. *sukkot*): Temporary dwelling reminiscent of the booths used by the ancient Israelites as they wandered in the desert.

Sukkot: Fall harvest festival marked by the construction of booths or huts, also known as *sukkot*.

tallit: Prayer shawl.

tamid: "Eternal"; often refers to the perpetual sacrifice in the ancient Temple cult. (The *ner tamid* is the "eternal light" in the front of the sanctuary that is a reminder of God's constant presence, and somewhat reminiscent of this ancient sacrifice.)

tevilah: Immersion in a ritual bath.

tikkun leyl Shavuot: All-night study on the evening of Shavuot.

tikkun olam: This term, which means "repair of a broken world," is borrowed from the mystical Lurianic myth (about the world shattering at creation and scattering holy sparks that need to be collected) and used as a general reference to social activism.

Torah: The parchment scroll on which are written the Five Books of Moses, the first five books of the Hebrew Scriptures.

tzedakah: Charitable giving.

tzimtzum: Literally, "contraction," referring to God contracting the Divine Self in order to make room for the creation of the world out of the Divine.

ulpan: Intensive Hebrew language immersion program.

Va'ad Harabbanim: The rabbinical body that oversees the granting of kosher licenses for restaurants and the like, generally made up only of Orthodox rabbis.

written law: An alternative way of referring to the Torah.

Yad Vashem: The Holocaust Memorial in Jerusalem.

Yerushalayim shel malah: "Heavenly Jerusalem."

Yerushalayim shel matah: "Earthly Jerusalem."

Yom Kippur: Day of Atonement; one of two so-called High Holidays that take place in the early fall. It occurs on the tenth day following Rosh Hashanah, and is observed by fasting and prayer.

yesh li: Hebrew for "mine," possession.

Resources for Further Study

ORGANIZATIONS

Kolot: The Center for Jewish Women and Gender Studies
1299 Church Rd.
Wyncote, PA 19095
(215) 576-0800
www.kolot.org
Located at the Reconstructionist Rabbinical College in the Philadelphia metropolitan area, this organization is devoted to the development of rituals that complement the life challenges that women face in their interface with Judaism and Jewish life.

Ma'yan: The Jewish Women's Project
334 Amsterdam Ave.
New York, NY 10023
(646) 505-4444
This is a pioneering Jewish women's organization that provides cutting-edge resources. It is housed at the JCC in Manhattan on New York's Upper West Side.

The Shefa Fund
8459 Ridge Ave.
Philadelphia, PA 19128
(215) 483-4004
www.shefafund.org
This is a liberal philanthropic fund with a social conscience. Of particular note is its "Torah as Money" program.

WEBSITES

TorahQuest
www.JRF.org/torahquest
A website sponsored by the Jewish Reconstructionist Federation for the study of Torah; exceptionally accessible. People can enter and participate at any level.

www.jewishculture.org
An exceptionally thorough website that provides easily accessible information on a wide variety of topics.

www.jewishmuseum.org
While there are Jewish museums in many cities across North America, this is the website for one of the oldest. It introduces visitors to the museum's extensive collection of Jewish ritual objects, as well as its changing exhibitions that focus on various aspects of Jewish life, art, and culture.

BOOKS

Edward Feinstein, *Tough Questions Jews Ask: A Young Adult's Guide to Building a Jewish Life.* Woodstock, Vt.: Jewish Lights Publishing, 2003.

    This conversational, engaging book shows that asking good

questions is a hallmark of Jewish spirituality. Wise but accessible, reverent but funny, Rabbi Edward Feinstein leaves no question unasked and no curiosity unaddressed.

Nancy Fuchs-Kreimer, *Parenting as a Spiritual Journey: Deepening Ordinary & Extraordinary Events into Sacred Occasions.* Woodstock, Vt.: Jewish Lights Publishing, 1998.

This is a helpful guide for anyone seeking to re-envision family life. It explores the transformative spiritual adventure that all parents can experience while bringing up their children and shows how even the seemingly insignificant moments in a day with your child can be infused with spiritual meaning. Rituals, prayers, and inspiring passages from sacred Jewish texts are woven throughout this insightful, enriching, and often amusing book.

Neil Gillman, *The Jewish Approach to God: A Brief Introduction for Christians.* Woodstock, Vt.: Jewish Lights Publishing, 2003.

Rabbi Neil Gillman guides Christians through the different ways the Jewish people have related to God, how each practice originated, and what each may mean for Christians and their understanding of their own faith. By exploring the Jewish ways of encountering God, Gillman helps all readers to understand what the search itself says about Jewish tradition and how people of all faiths can draw on the fundamentals of Judaism to strengthen, explore, and deepen their own spiritual foundations.

Arthur Green, *These Are the Words: A Vocabulary of a Jewish Spiritual Life.* Woodstock, Vt.: Jewish Lights Publishing, 1999.

This comprehensive guide addresses the meaning, history, and origin of the core 149 Hebrew words that are shared and understood throughout the Jewish world.

Morris Kertzer, *What Is a Jew?* Revised by Lawrence Hoffman. New York: Touchstone Books, 1997.

This is a classic introduction to Judaism, revised and issued anew by the author's nephew, who is a prominent liturgist and member of the faculty at Hebrew Union College–Jewish Institute of Religion, the academic center of the Reform movement in New York.

Lawrence Kushner, *Jewish Spirituality: A Brief Introduction for Christians.* Woodstock, Vt.: Jewish Lights Publishing, 2001.

Rabbi Lawrence Kushner introduces readers to the Talmud, Midrash, and mystical and biblical stories. He reveals the essence of Judaism in a way that people whose own tradition traces its roots to Judaism can understand and enjoy.

Stuart M. Matlins, ed., *The Jewish Lights Spirituality Handbook: A Guide to Understanding, Exploring, and Living a Spiritual Life.* Woodstock, Vt.: Jewish Lights Publishing, 2001.

Fifty prominent spiritual leaders invite readers to explore every aspect of Jewish spirituality—God, community, prayer, liturgy, healing, meditation, mysticism, study, Jewish traditions, rituals, blessings, life passages, special days, the everyday, repairing the world, and more—offering in one place everything you need to discover all the directions that Jewish spirituality can go and take you.

The New Jewish Baby Album: Creating and Celebrating the Beginning of a Spiritual Life—A Jewish Lights Companion. Woodstock, Vt.: Jewish Lights Publishing, 2003.

More than just a memory book, *The New Jewish Baby Album* shows you how—and why it's important—to create a Jewish home and a Jewish life. It includes a place to describe the naming ceremony, space to write affirmations, and pages for writing original blessings and creating original prayers, as well as meaningful quotes throughout.

Kerry M. Olitzky and Ronald Isaacs, *The "How to" Handbooks for Jewish Living*, 3 volumes. Hoboken, N.J.: KTAV, 1993–2002.

These three volumes primarily focus on the functional aspects of Jewish ritual. While the authors note the sources for each ritual, they avoid any discussion at all. The format is easily accessible and friendly.

Kerry M. Olitzky and Daniel Judson, *The Rituals & Practices of a Jewish Life: A Handbook for Personal Spiritual Renewal.* Woodstock, Vt.: Jewish Lights Publishing, 2002.

This guide features inspiring, practical information and advice to enrich a Jewish spiritual life with traditional rituals and practices. Each chapter explores a different ritual or practice in depth and explains why do it, what to do, and how to do it.

Kerry M. Olitzky with Joan Peterson Littman, *Making a Successful Jewish Interfaith Marriage: The Jewish Outreach Institute Guide to Opportunities, Challenges and Resources.* Woodstock, Vt.: Jewish Lights Publishing, 2003.

From a Jewish perspective, this book guides interfaith couples at any stage of their relationship—from dating, engagement, and the wedding to the marriage—and the people who are affected by their relationship in any way, including their families and counselors who work with interfaith couples.

Judea and Ruth Pearl, *I Am Jewish: Personal Reflections Inspired by the Last Words of Daniel Pearl.* Woodstock, Vt.: Jewish Lights Publishing, 2004.

Based on the last words of *Wall Street Journal* reporter Daniel Pearl—who was murdered by terrorists in Pakistan—*I Am Jewish* examines what this short statement means to Jewish people from all walks of life, from all around the world, in their own words. One hundred forty-seven contributors—both famous Jews and average citizens—from twelve countries express what being Jewish means to them.

Zalman M. Schachter-Shalomi, *First Steps to a New Jewish Spirit: Reb Zalman's Guide to Recapturing the Intimacy & Ecstasy in Your Relationship with God.* Woodstock, Vt.: Jewish Lights Publishing, 2003.

This extraordinary spiritual handbook restores psychic and physical vigor by introducing readers to new models and alternative ways of practicing Judaism. Breaking free from traditional, formulaic ways of Jewish worship, it offers meditation and contemplation exercises for enriching the most important aspects of everyday life.

Richard Siegel, Michael Strassfeld, and Sharon Strassfeld. *The Jewish Catalogue, vols. 1–2.* Philadelphia: Jewish Publication Society, 1976.

These volumes are the Jewish response to the *Whole Earth Catalogue,* which shaped an entire generation in the late 1960s and early 1970s.

Ron Wolfson, *The Art of Jewish Living* series. Woodstock, Vt.: Jewish Lights Publishing.

This series contains four volumes, all focusing on important elements of Jewish ritual life. They provide easy access and profound insights, as well as clear and concise "how to" instructions. Titles include: *Passover: The Family Guide to Spiritual Celebration; Hanukkah: The Family Guide to Spiritual Celebration; Shabbat: The Family Guide to Preparing for and Celebrating the Sabbath; A*

Time to Mourn, A Time to Comfort: A Guide to Jewish Bereavement and Comfort. Workbooks and audiocassettes are also available.

MAGAZINES AND NEWSPAPERS

The Forward
45 E. 33rd St.
New York, NY 10016-5336
(212) 899-8200
www.forward.com
Originally serving the Yiddish-speaking community, this newspaper, now published in English, is considered to represent the "intellectual" interests of the Jewish community.

Hadassah
50 W. 58th St.
New York, NY 10019-2505
(212) 688-0277
www.hadassah.org
A publication of the largest Jewish women's organization, whose primary mission is support for the State of Israel.

The (New York) Jewish Week
1501 Broadway, Ste. 505
New York, NY 10036
(212) 921-7822
www.thejewishweek.com
While regional in nature, this has become the Jewish community's national newspaper of record.

Lilith
250 W. 57th St., Ste 2432
New York, NY 10107
(212) 757-0818
www.lilithmag.com
A Jewish feminist journal.

Moment
4710-41st St. NW
Washington, DC 20016
(202) 364-3300
www.momentmag.com
A popular magazine that features various perspectives on Jewish life and living.

Tikkun
2342 Shattuck Ave., Ste. 1200
San Francisco, CA 94109
(510) 644-1200
www.tikkun.org
A liberal magazine that focuses on issues of social justice.

Children's Books

Because Nothing Looks Like God
By Lawrence and Karen Kushner
What is God like? The first collaborative work by husband-and-wife team Lawrence and Karen Kushner introduces children to the possibilities of spiritual life. Real-life examples of happiness and sadness invite us to explore, together with our children, the questions we all have about God, no matter what our age.
11 x 8½, 32 pp, Full-color illus., Hardcover, ISBN 1-58023-092-X **$16.95** *For ages 4 & up*

Also Available: **Because Nothing Looks Like God Teacher's Guide**
8½ x 11, 22 pp, PB, ISBN 1-58023-140-3 **$6.95** *For ages 5–8*

Board Book Companions to *Because Nothing Looks Like God*
5 x 5, 24 pp, Full-color illus., SkyLight Paths Board Books, **$7.95** each *For ages 0–4*

What Does God Look Like? ISBN 1-893361-23-3
How Does God Make Things Happen? ISBN 1-893361-24-1
Where Is God? ISBN 1-893361-17-9

The 11th Commandment: Wisdom from Our Children
by The Children of America
"If there were an Eleventh Commandment, what would it be?" Children of many religious denominations across America answer this question—in their own drawings and words.
8 x 10, 48 pp, Full-color illus., Hardcover, ISBN 1-879045-46-X **$16.95** *For all ages*

Jerusalem of Gold: Jewish Stories of the Enchanted City
Retold by Howard Schwartz. Full-color illus. by Neil Waldman.
A beautiful and engaging collection of historical and legendary stories for children. Each celebrates the magical city that has served as a beacon for the Jewish imagination for three thousand years. Draws on Talmud, midrash, Jewish folklore, and mystical and Hasidic sources.
8 x 10, 64 pp, Full-color illus., Hardcover, ISBN 1-58023-149-7 **$18.95** *For ages 7 & up*

The Book of Miracles: A Young Person's Guide to Jewish Spiritual Awareness
By Lawrence Kushner. All-new illustrations by the author.
6 x 9, 96 pp, 2-color illus., Hardcover, ISBN 1-879045-78-8 **$16.95** *For ages 9–13*

In Our Image: God's First Creatures
By Nancy Sohn Swartz
9 x 12, 32 pp, Full-color illus., Hardcover, ISBN 1-879045-99-0 **$16.95** *For ages 4 & up*

From SKYLIGHT PATHS PUBLISHING

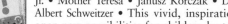

Becoming Me: A Story of Creation
By Martin Boroson. Full-color illus. by Christopher Gilvan-Cartwright.
Told in the personal "voice" of the Creator, a story about creation and relationship that is about each one of us. In simple words and with radiant illustrations, the Creator tells an intimate story about love, about friendship and playing, about our world—and about ourselves.
8 x 10, 32 pp, Full-color illus., Hardcover, ISBN 1-893361-11-X **$16.95** *For ages 4 & up*

Ten Amazing People: And How They Changed the World
By Maura D. Shaw. Foreword by Dr. Robert Coles. Full-color illus. by Stephen Marchesi.
Black Elk • Dorothy Day • Malcolm X • Mahatma Gandhi • Martin Luther King, Jr. • Mother Teresa • Janusz Korczak • Desmond Tutu • Thich Nhat Hanh • Albert Schweitzer • This vivid, inspirational, and authoritative book will open new possibilities for children by telling the stories of how ten of the past century's greatest leaders changed the world in important ways.
8½ x 11, 48 pp, Full-color illus., Hardcover, ISBN 1-893361-47-0 **$17.95** *For ages 7 & up*

Where Does God Live? *By August Gold and Matthew J. Perlman*
Using simple, everyday examples that children can relate to, this colorful book helps young readers develop a personal understanding of God.
10 x 8½ , 32 pp, Full-color photo illus., Quality PB, ISBN 1-893361-39-X **$8.99** *For ages 3–6*

Abraham Joshua Heschel

The Earth Is the Lord's: The Inner World of the Jew in Eastern Europe
5½ x 8, 128 pp, Quality PB, ISBN 1-879045-42-7 **$14.95**

Israel: An Echo of Eternity *New Introduction by Susannah Heschel*
5½ x 8, 272 pp, Quality PB, ISBN 1-879045-70-2 **$19.95**

A Passion for Truth: Despair and Hope in Hasidism
5½ x 8, 352 pp, Quality PB, ISBN 1-879045-41-9 **$18.99**

Holidays/Holy Days

7th Heaven: Celebrating Shabbat with Rebbe Nachman of Breslov
By Moshe Mykoff with the Breslov Research Institute
Based on the teachings of Rebbe Nachman of Breslov. Explores the art of consciously observing Shabbat and understanding in-depth many of the day's traditional spiritual practices.
5⅛ x 8¼, 224 pp, Deluxe PB w/flaps, ISBN 1-58023-175-6 **$18.95**

The Women's Passover Companion
Women's Reflections on the Festival of Freedom
Edited by Rabbi Sharon Cohen Anisfeld, Tara Mohr, and Catherine Spector
A groundbreaking collection that captures the voices of Jewish women who engage in a provocative conversation about women's relationships to Passover as well as the roots and meanings of women's seders.
6 x 9, 352 pp, Hardcover, ISBN 1-58023-128-4 **$24.95**

The Women's Seder Sourcebook
Rituals & Readings for Use at the Passover Seder
Edited by Rabbi Sharon Cohen Anisfeld, Tara Mohr, and Catherine Spector
This practical guide gathers the voices of more than one hundred women in readings, personal and creative reflections, commentaries, blessings, and ritual suggestions that can be incorporated into your Passover celebration as supplements to or substitutes for traditional passages of the haggadah.
6 x 9, 384 pp, Hardcover, ISBN 1-58023-136-5 **$24.95**

Creating Lively Passover Seders: A Sourcebook of Engaging Tales, Texts & Activities
By David Arnow, Ph.D.
7 x 9, 416 pp, Quality PB, ISBN 1-58023-184-5 **$24.99**

Hanukkah, 2nd Edition: The Family Guide to Spiritual Celebration
By Dr. Ron Wolfson. Edited by Joel Lurie Grishaver.
7 x 9, 240 pp, illus., Quality PB, ISBN 1-58023-122-5 **$18.95**

The Jewish Family Fun Book: Holiday Projects, Everyday Activities, and Travel Ideas with Jewish Themes *By Danielle Dardashti and Roni Sarig. Illus. by Avi Katz.*
6 x 9, 288 pp, 70+ b/w illus. & diagrams, Quality PB, ISBN 1-58023-171-3 **$18.95**

The Jewish Gardening Cookbook: Growing Plants & Cooking for
Holidays & Festivals *By Michael Brown*
6 x 9, 224 pp, 30+ illus., Quality PB, ISBN 1-58023-116-0 **$16.95**;
Hardcover, ISBN 1-58023-004-0 **$21.95**

Passover, 2nd Edition: The Family Guide to Spiritual Celebration
By Dr. Ron Wolfson with Joel Lurie Grishaver
7 x 9, 352 pp, Quality PB, ISBN 1-58023-174-8 **$19.95**

Shabbat, 2nd Edition: The Family Guide to Preparing for and Celebrating the Sabbath
By Dr. Ron Wolfson 7 x 9, 320 pp, illus., Quality PB, ISBN 1-58023-164-0 **$19.95**

Sharing Blessings: Children's Stories for Exploring the Spirit of the Jewish Holidays
By Rahel Musleah and Michael Klayman
8½ x 11, 64 pp, Full-color illus., Hardcover, ISBN 1-879045-71-0 **$18.95** *For ages 6 & up*

Inspiration

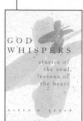

God in All Moments
Mystical & Practical Spiritual Wisdom from Hasidic Masters
Edited and translated by Or N. Rose with Ebn D. Leader
Hasidic teachings on how to be mindful in religious practice and how to cultivate everyday ethical behavior—*hanhagot*. 5½ x 8½, 192 pp, Quality PB, ISBN 1-58023-186-1 **$16.95**

Our Dance with God: Finding Prayer, Perspective and Meaning in the Stories of Our Lives *By Karyn D. Kedar* 6 x 9, 176 pp, Quality PB, ISBN 1-58023-202-7 **$16.99**

Also Available: **The Dance of the Dolphin** (Hardcover edition of *Our Dance with God*)
6 x 9, 176 pp, Hardcover, ISBN 1-58023-154-3 **$19.95**

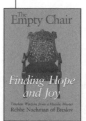

The Empty Chair: Finding Hope and Joy—Timeless Wisdom from a Hasidic Master, Rebbe Nachman of Breslov *Adapted by Moshe Mykoff and the Breslov Research Institute*
4 x 6, 128 pp, 2-color text, Deluxe PB w/flaps, ISBN 1-879045-67-2 **$9.95**

The Gentle Weapon: Prayers for Everyday and Not-So-Everyday Moments—Timeless Wisdom from the Teachings of the Hasidic Master, Rebbe Nachman of Breslov *Adapted by Moshe Mykoff and S. C. Mizrahi, together with the Breslov Research Institute*
4 x 6, 144 pp, 2-color text, Deluxe PB w/flaps, ISBN 1-58023-022-9 **$9.95**

God Whispers: Stories of the Soul, Lessons of the Heart *By Karyn D. Kedar*
6 x 9, 176 pp, Quality PB, ISBN 1-58023-088-1 **$15.95**

An Orphan in History: One Man's Triumphant Search for His Jewish Roots *By Paul Cowan. Afterword by Rachel Cowan.* 6 x 9, 288 pp, Quality PB, ISBN 1-58023-135-7 **$16.95**

Restful Reflections: Nighttime Inspiration to Calm the Soul, Based on Jewish Wisdom *By Rabbi Kerry M. Olitzky & Rabbi Lori Forman*
4½ x 6½, 448 pp, Quality PB, ISBN 1-58023-091-1 **$15.95**

Sacred Intentions: Daily Inspiration to Strengthen the Spirit, Based on Jewish Wisdom *By Rabbi Kerry M. Olitzky and Rabbi Lori Forman*
4½ x 6½, 448 pp, Quality PB, ISBN 1-58023-061-X **$15.95**

Kabbalah/Mysticism/Enneagram

Seek My Face: A Jewish Mystical Theology
By Dr. Arthur Green
This classic work of contemporary Jewish theology, revised and updated, is a profound, deeply personal statement of the lasting truths of Jewish mysticism and the basic faith claims of Judaism. A tool for anyone seeking the elusive presence of God in the world. 6 x 9, 304 pp, Quality PB, ISBN 1-58023-130-6 **$19.95**

Zohar: Annotated & Explained
Translation and annotation by Dr. Daniel C. Matt. Foreword by Andrew Harvey, SkyLight Illuminations series editor.
Offers insightful yet unobtrusive commentary to the masterpiece of Jewish mysticism that explains references and mystical symbols, shares wisdom of spiritual masters, and clarifies the *Zohar*'s bold claim: We have always been taught that we need God, but in order to manifest in the world, God needs us.
5½ x 8½, 160 pp, Quality PB, ISBN 1-893361-51-9 **$15.99** *(A SkyLight Paths book)*

Cast in God's Image: Discover Your Personality Type Using the Enneagram and Kabbalah *By Rabbi Howard A. Addison*
7 x 9, 176 pp, Quality PB, Layflat binding, 20+ journaling exercises, ISBN 1-58023-124-1 **$16.95**

Ehyeh: A Kabbalah for Tomorrow *By Dr. Arthur Green*
6 x 9, 224 pp, Hardcover, ISBN 1-58023-125-X **$21.99**

The Enneagram and Kabbalah: Reading Your Soul *By Rabbi Howard A. Addison*
6 x 9, 176 pp, Quality PB, ISBN 1-58023-001-6 **$15.95**

Finding Joy: A Practical Spiritual Guide to Happiness *By Dannel I. Schwartz with Mark Hass*
6 x 9, 192 pp, Quality PB, ISBN 1-58023-009-1 **$14.95**; Hardcover, ISBN 1-879045-53-2 **$19.95**

The Gift of Kabbalah: Discovering the Secrets of Heaven, Renewing Your Life on Earth *By Tamar Frankiel, Ph.D.*
6 x 9, 256 pp, Quality PB, ISBN 1-58023-141-1 **$16.95**; Hardcover, ISBN 1-58023-108-X **$21.95**

The Way Into Jewish Mystical Tradition *By Lawrence Kushner*
6 x 9, 224 pp, Quality PB, ISBN 1-58023-200-0 **$18.99**; Hardcover, ISBN 1-58023-029-6 **$21.95**

Life Cycle
Parenting

The New Jewish Baby Album: Creating and Celebrating the Beginning of a Spiritual Life—A Jewish Lights Companion
By the Editors at Jewish Lights. Foreword by Anita Diamant. Preface by Sandy Eisenberg Sasso.
A spiritual keepsake that will be treasured for generations. More than just a memory book, *shows you how—and why it's important*—to create a Jewish home and a Jewish life. Includes sections to describe naming ceremony, space to write encouragements, and pages for writing original blessings, prayers, and meaningful quotes throughout.
8 x 10, 64 pp, Deluxe Padded Hardcover, Full-color illus., ISBN 1-58023-138-1 **$19.95**

The Jewish Pregnancy Book: A Resource for the Soul, Body & Mind during Pregnancy, Birth & the First Three Months
By Sandy Falk, M.D., and Rabbi Daniel Judson, with Steven A. Rapp
Includes medical information on fetal development, pre-natal testing and more, from a liberal Jewish perspective; prenatal *Aleph-Bet* yoga; and ancient and modern prayers and rituals for each stage of pregnancy.
7 x 10, 208 pp, Quality PB, b/w illus., ISBN 1-58023-178-0 **$16.95**

Celebrating Your New Jewish Daughter: Creating Jewish Ways to Welcome Baby Girls into the Covenant—New and Traditional Ceremonies
By Debra Nussbaum Cohen 6 x 9, 272 pp, Quality PB, ISBN 1-58023-090-3 **$18.95**

The New Jewish Baby Book: Names, Ceremonies & Customs—A Guide for Today's Families *By Anita Diamant* 6 x 9, 336 pp, Quality PB, ISBN 1-879045-28-1 **$18.95**

Parenting As a Spiritual Journey: Deepening Ordinary and Extraordinary Events into Sacred Occasions *By Rabbi Nancy Fuchs-Kreimer*
6 x 9, 224 pp, Quality PB, ISBN 1-58023-016-4 **$16.95**

Embracing the Covenant: Converts to Judaism Talk About Why & How
Edited and with introductions by Rabbi Allan Berkowitz and Patti Moskovitz
6 x 9, 192 pp, Quality PB, ISBN 1-879045-50-8 **$16.95**

The Guide to Jewish Interfaith Family Life: An InterfaithFamily.com Handbook
Edited by Ronnie Friedland and Edmund Case 6 x 9, 384 pp, Quality PB, ISBN 1-58023-153-5 **$18.95**

Making a Successful Jewish Interfaith Marriage: The Jewish Outreach Institute Guide to Opportunities, Challenges and Resources
By Rabbi Kerry Olitzky with Joan Peterson Littman 6 x 9, 176 pp, Quality PB, ISBN 1-58023-170-5 **$16.95**

The Perfect Stranger's Guide to Wedding Ceremonies
A Guide to Etiquette in Other People's Religious Ceremonies *Edited by Stuart M. Matlins*
6 x 9, 208 pp, Quality PB, ISBN 1-893361-19-5 **$16.95** *(A SkyLight Paths book)*

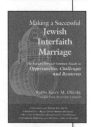

How to Be a Perfect Stranger, 3rd Edition
The Essential Religious Etiquette Handbook
Edited by Stuart M. Matlins and Arthur J. Magida
The indispensable guidebook to help the well-meaning guest when visiting other people's religious ceremonies.
  A straightforward guide to the rituals and celebrations of the major religions and denominations in the United States and Canada from the perspective of an interested guest of any other faith, based on information obtained from authorities of each religion. Belongs in every living room, library, and office.
6 x 9, 432 pp, Quality PB, ISBN 1-893361-67-5 **$19.95** *(A SkyLight Paths book)*

Divorce Is a Mitzvah: A Practical Guide to Finding Wholeness and Holiness When Your Marriage Dies *By Rabbi Perry Netter. Afterword by Rabbi Laura Geller.*
6 x 9, 224 pp, Quality PB, ISBN 1-58023-172-1 **$16.95**

A Heart of Wisdom: Making the Jewish Journey from Midlife through the Elder Years
Edited by Susan Berrin. Foreword by Harold Kushner. 6 x 9, 384 pp, Quality PB, ISBN 1-58023-051-2 **$18.95**

So That Your Values Live On: Ethical Wills and How to Prepare Them
Edited by Jack Riemer and Nathaniel Stampfer 6 x 9, 272 pp, Quality PB, ISBN 1-879045-34-6 **$18.95**

Meditation

The Handbook of Jewish Meditation Practices
A Guide for Enriching the Sabbath and Other Days of Your Life
By Rabbi David A. Cooper
Easy-to-learn meditation techniques for use on the Sabbath and every day, to help us return to the roots of traditional Jewish spirituality where Shabbat is a state of mind and soul. 6 x 9, 208 pp, Quality PB, ISBN 1-58023-102-0 **$16.95**

Discovering Jewish Meditation: Instruction & Guidance for Learning an Ancient
Spiritual Practice By Nan Fink Gefen, Ph.D. 6 x 9, 208 pp, Quality PB, ISBN 1-58023-067-9 **$16.95**

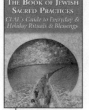

A Heart of Stillness: A Complete Guide to Learning the Art of Meditation
By Rabbi David A. Cooper
5½ x 8½, 272 pp, Quality PB, ISBN 1-893361-03-9 **$16.95** (A SkyLight Paths book)

Meditation from the Heart of Judaism: Today's Teachers Share Their
Practices, Techniques, and Faith Edited by Avram Davis
6 x 9, 256 pp, Quality PB, ISBN 1-58023-049-0 **$16.95**

Silence, Simplicity & Solitude: A Complete Guide to Spiritual Retreat at Home
By Rabbi David A. Cooper
5½ x 8½, 336 pp, Quality PB, ISBN 1-893361-04-7 **$16.95** (A SkyLight Paths book)

Three Gates to Meditation Practice: A Personal Journey into Sufism,
Buddhism, and Judaism By Rabbi David A. Cooper
5½ x 8½, 240 pp, Quality PB, ISBN 1-893361-22-5 **$16.95** (A SkyLight Paths book)

The Way of Flame: A Guide to the Forgotten Mystical Tradition of Jewish Meditation
By Avram Davis 4½ x 8, 176 pp, Quality PB, ISBN 1-58023-060-1 **$15.95**

Ritual/Sacred Practice

The Jewish Dream Book
The Key to Opening the Inner Meaning of Your Dreams
By Vanessa L. Ochs with Elizabeth Ochs; Full-color Illus. by Kristina Swarner
Vibrant illustrations, instructions for how modern people can perform ancient Jewish dream practices, and dream interpretations drawn from the Jewish wisdom tradition help make this guide the ideal bedside companion for anyone who wants to further their understanding of their dreams—and themselves.
8 x 8, 120 pp, Full-color illus., Deluxe PB w/flaps, ISBN 1-58023-132-2 **$16.95**

The Rituals & Practices of a Jewish Life: A Handbook for Personal Spiritual
Renewal Edited by Rabbi Kerry M. Olitzky and Rabbi Daniel Judson
6 x 9, 272 pp, illus., Quality PB, ISBN 1-58023-169-1 **$18.95**

The Book of Jewish Sacred Practices: CLAL's Guide to Everyday & Holiday
Rituals & Blessings Edited by Rabbi Irwin Kula and Vanessa L. Ochs, Ph.D.
6 x 9, 368 pp, Quality PB, ISBN 1-58023-152-7 **$18.95**

Science Fiction/
Mystery & Detective Fiction

Mystery Midrash: An Anthology of Jewish Mystery & Detective Fiction
Edited by Lawrence W. Raphael. Preface by Joel Siegel.
6 x 9, 304 pp, Quality PB, ISBN 1-58023-055-5 **$16.95**

Criminal Kabbalah: An Intriguing Anthology of Jewish Mystery & Detective Fiction
Edited by Lawrence W. Raphael. Foreword by Laurie R. King.
6 x 9, 256 pp, Quality PB, ISBN 1-58023-109-8 **$16.95**

More Wandering Stars: An Anthology of Outstanding Stories of Jewish Fantasy and
Science Fiction Edited by Jack Dann. Introduction by Isaac Asimov.
6 x 9, 192 pp, Quality PB, ISBN 1-58023-063-6 **$16.95**

Wandering Stars: An Anthology of Jewish Fantasy & Science Fiction
Edited by Jack Dann. Introduction by Isaac Asimov.
6 x 9, 272 pp, Quality PB, ISBN 1-58023-005-9 **$16.95**

Spirituality

The Alphabet of Paradise: An A–Z of Spirituality for Everyday Life
By Rabbi Howard Cooper
In twenty-six engaging chapters, Cooper spiritually illuminates the subjects of our daily lives—A to Z—examining these sources by using an ancient Jewish mystical method of interpretation that reveals both the literal and more allusive meanings of each. 5 x 7¾, 224 pp, Quality PB, ISBN 1-893361-80-2 **$16.95** *(A SkyLight Paths book)*

Does the Soul Survive?: A Jewish Journey to Belief in Afterlife, Past
Lives & Living with Purpose   *By Rabbi Elie Kaplan Spitz. Foreword by Brian L Weiss, M.D.*
Spitz relates his own experiences and those shared with him by people he has worked with as a rabbi, and shows us that belief in afterlife and past lives, so often approached with reluctance, is in fact true to Jewish tradition.
6 x 9, 288 pp, Quality PB, ISBN 1-58023-165-9 **$16.95**; Hardcover, ISBN 1-58023-094-6 **$21.95**

First Steps to a New Jewish Spirit: Reb Zalman's Guide to
Recapturing the Intimacy & Ecstasy in Your Relationship with God
By Rabbi Zalman M. Schachter-Shalomi with Donald Gropman
An extraordinary spiritual handbook that restores psychic and physical vigor by introducing us to new models and alternative ways of practicing Judaism. Offers meditation and contemplation exercises for enriching the most important aspects of everyday life.   6 x 9, 144 pp, Quality PB, ISBN 1-58023-182-9 **$16.95**

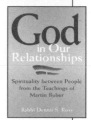

God in Our Relationships: Spirituality between People from the
Teachings of Martin Buber   *By Rabbi Dennis S. Ross*
On the eightieth anniversary of Buber's classic work, we can discover new answers to critical issues in our lives. Inspiring examples from Ross's own life—as congregational rabbi, father, hospital chaplain, social worker, and husband—illustrate Buber's difficult-to-understand ideas about how we encounter God and each other. 5½ x 8½, 160 pp, Quality PB, ISBN 1-58023-147-0 **$16.95**

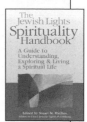

The Jewish Lights Spirituality Handbook: A Guide to Understanding,
Exploring & Living a Spiritual Life   *Edited by Stuart M. Matlins*
What exactly is "Jewish" about spirituality? How do I make it a part of my life? Fifty of today's foremost spiritual leaders share their ideas and experience with us.
6 x 9, 456 pp, Quality PB, ISBN 1-58023-093-8 **$19.99**; Hardcover, ISBN 1-58023-100-4 **$24.95**

Bringing the Psalms to Life: How to Understand and Use the Book of Psalms
By Dr. Daniel F. Polish
6 x 9, 208 pp, Quality PB, ISBN 1-58023-157-8 **$16.95**; Hardcover, ISBN 1-58023-077-6 **$21.95**

God & the Big Bang: Discovering Harmony between Science & Spirituality
By Dr. Daniel C. Matt 6 x 9, 216 pp, Quality PB, ISBN 1-879045-89-3 **$16.95**

Godwrestling—Round 2: Ancient Wisdom, Future Paths
By Rabbi Arthur Waskow 6 x 9, 352 pp, Quality PB, ISBN 1-879045-72-9 **$18.95**

One God Clapping: The Spiritual Path of a Zen Rabbi   *By Rabbi Alan Lew with Sherril Jaffe*
5½ x 8½, 336 pp, Quality PB, ISBN 1-58023-115-2 **$16.95**

The Path of Blessing: Experiencing the Energy and Abundance of the Divine
By Rabbi Marcia Prager 5½ x 8½, 240 pp., Quality PB, ISBN 1-58023-148-9 **$16.95**

Six Jewish Spiritual Paths: A Rationalist Looks at Spirituality   *By Rabbi Rifat Sonsino*
6 x 9, 208 pp, Quality PB, ISBN 1-58023-167-5 **$16.95**; Hardcover, ISBN 1-58023-095-4 **$21.95**

Soul Judaism: Dancing with God into a New Era
By Rabbi Wayne Dosick 5½ x 8½, 304 pp, Quality PB, ISBN 1-58023-053-9 **$16.95**

Stepping Stones to Jewish Spiritual Living: Walking the Path Morning, Noon,
and Night *By Rabbi James L. Mirel and Karen Bonnell Werth*
6 x 9, 240 pp, Quality PB, ISBN 1-58023-074-1 **$16.95**; Hardcover, ISBN 1-58023-003-2 **$21.95**

There Is No Messiah... and You're It: The Stunning Transformation of Judaism's
Most Provocative Idea *By Rabbi Robert N. Levine, D.D.*
6 x 9, 192 pp, Hardcover, ISBN 1-58023-173-X **$21.95**

These Are the Words: A Vocabulary of Jewish Spiritual Life   *By Dr. Arthur Green*
6 x 9, 304 pp, Quality PB, ISBN 1-58023-107-1 **$18.95**

Spirituality/Lawrence Kushner

The Book of Letters: A Mystical Hebrew Alphabet
Popular Hardcover Edition, 6 x 9, 80 pp, 2-color text, ISBN 1-879045-00-1 **$24.95**
Deluxe Gift Edition with slipcase, 9 x 12, 80 pp, 4-color text, Hardcover, ISBN 1-879045-01-X **$79.95**
Collector's Limited Edition, 9 x 12, 80 pp, gold foil embossed pages, w/limited edition silkscreened
print, ISBN 1-879045-04-4 **$349.00**

The Book of Miracles: A Young Person's Guide to Jewish Spiritual Awareness
All-new illustrations by the author
6 x 9, 96 pp, 2-color illus., Hardcover, ISBN 1-879045-78-8 **$16.95** *For ages 9–13*

The Book of Words: Talking Spiritual Life, Living Spiritual Talk
6 x 9, 160 pp, Quality PB, ISBN 1-58023-020-2 **$16.95**

Eyes Remade for Wonder: A Lawrence Kushner Reader
Introduction by Thomas Moore
6 x 9, 240 pp, Quality PB, ISBN 1-58023-042-3 **$18.95;** Hardcover, ISBN 1-58023-014-8 **$23.95**

God Was in This Place & I, i Did Not Know
Finding Self, Spirituality and Ultimate Meaning
6 x 9, 192 pp, Quality PB, ISBN 1-879045-33-8 **$16.95**

Honey from the Rock: An Introduction to Jewish Mysticism
6 x 9, 176 pp, Quality PB, ISBN 1-58023-073-3 **$16.95**

Invisible Lines of Connection: Sacred Stories of the Ordinary
5½ x 8½, 160 pp, Quality PB, ISBN 1-879045-98-2 **$15.95**

Jewish Spirituality—A Brief Introduction for Christians
5½ x 8½, 112 pp, Quality PB Original, ISBN 1-58023-150-0 **$12.95**

The River of Light: Jewish Mystical Awareness
6 x 9, 192 pp, Quality PB, ISBN 1-58023-096-2 **$16.95**

The Way Into Jewish Mystical Tradition
6 x 9, 224 pp, Quality PB, ISBN 1-58023-200-0 **$18.99;** Hardcover, ISBN 1-58023-029-6 **$21.95**

Spirituality/Prayer

Pray Tell: A Hadassah Guide to Jewish Prayer
By Rabbi Jules Harlow, with contributions from Tamara Cohen, Rochelle Furstenberg, Rabbi Daniel Gordis, Leora Tanenbaum, and many others
A guide to traditional Jewish prayer enriched with insight and wisdom from a broad variety of viewpoints—from Orthodox, Conservative, Reform, and Reconstructionist Judaism to New Age and feminist. Offers fresh and modern slants on what it means to pray as a Jew, and how women and men might actually pray. 8½ x 11, 400 pp, Quality PB, ISBN 1-58023-163-2 **$29.95**

My People's Prayer Book Series
Traditional Prayers, Modern Commentaries
Edited by Rabbi Lawrence A. Hoffman
Provides diverse and exciting commentary to the traditional liturgy, helping modern men and women find new wisdom in Jewish prayer, and bring liturgy into their lives.

Each book includes Hebrew text, modern translation, and commentaries from all perspectives of the Jewish world.
Vol. 1—The *Sh'ma* and Its Blessings
7 x 10, 168 pp, Hardcover, ISBN 1-879045-79-6 **$23.95**
Vol. 2—The *Amidah*
7 x 10, 240 pp, Hardcover, ISBN 1-879045-80-X **$24.95**
Vol. 3—*P'sukei D'zimrah* (Morning Psalms)
7 x 10, 240 pp, Hardcover, ISBN 1-879045-81-8 **$24.95**
Vol. 4—*Seder K'riat Hatorah* (The Torah Service)
7 x 10, 264 pp, Hardcover, ISBN 1-879045-82-6 **$23.95**
Vol. 5—*Birkhot Hashachar* (Morning Blessings)
7 x 10, 240 pp, Hardcover, ISBN 1-879045-83-4 **$24.95**
Vol. 6—*Tachanun* and Concluding Prayers
7 x 10, 240 pp, Hardcover, ISBN 1-879045-84-2 **$24.95**
Vol. 7—Shabbat at Home
7 x 10, 240 pp, Hardcover, ISBN 1-879045-85-0 **$24.95**

Spirituality/The Way Into... Series

The Way Into... Series offers an accessible and highly usable "guided tour" of the Jewish faith, people, history and beliefs—in total, an introduction to Judaism that will enable you to understand and interact with the sacred texts of the Jewish tradition. Each volume is written by a leading contemporary scholar and teacher, and explores one key aspect of Judaism. *The Way Into...* enables all readers to achieve a real sense of Jewish cultural literacy through guided study.

The Way Into Encountering God in Judaism *By Neil Gillman*
6 x 9, 240 pp, Quality PB, ISBN 1-58023-199-3 **$18.99**; Hardcover, ISBN 1-58023-025-3 **$21.95**

Also Available: **The Jewish Approach to God: A Brief Introduction for Christians**
By Neil Gillman 5½ x 8½, 192 pp, Quality PB, ISBN 1-58023-190-X **$16.95**

The Way Into Jewish Mystical Tradition *By Lawrence Kushner*
6 x 9, 224 pp, Quality PB, ISBN 1-58023-200-0 **$18.99**; Hardcover, ISBN 1-58023-029-6 **$21.95**

The Way Into Jewish Prayer *By Lawrence A. Hoffman*
6 x 9, 224 pp, Quality PB, ISBN 1-58023-201-9 **$18.99**; Hardcover, ISBN 1-58023-027-X **$21.95**

The Way Into Torah *By Norman J. Cohen*
6 x 9, 176 pp, Quality PB, ISBN 1-58023-198-5 **$16.99**; Hardcover, ISBN 1-58023-028-8 **$21.95**

Spirituality in the Workplace

Being God's Partner
How to Find the Hidden Link Between Spirituality and Your Work
By Rabbi Jeffrey K. Salkin. Introduction by Norman Lear.
6 x 9, 192 pp, Quality PB, ISBN 1-879045-65-6 **$17.95**

The Business Bible: 10 New Commandments for Bringing Spirituality & Ethical
Values into the Workplace *By Rabbi Wayne Dosick*
5½ x 8½, 208 pp, Quality PB, ISBN 1-58023-101-2 **$14.95**

Spirituality and Wellness

Aleph-Bet Yoga
Embodying the Hebrew Letters for Physical and Spiritual Well-Being
By Steven A. Rapp. Foreword by Tamar Frankiel, Ph.D., and Judy Greenfeld. Preface by Hart Lazer
7 x 10, 128 pp, b/w photos, Quality PB, Layflat binding, ISBN 1-58023-162-4 **$16.95**

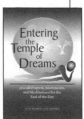

Entering the Temple of Dreams
Jewish Prayers, Movements, and Meditations for the End of the Day
By Tamar Frankiel, Ph.D., and Judy Greenfeld
7 x 10, 192 pp, illus., Quality PB, ISBN 1-58023-079-2 **$16.95**

Minding the Temple of the Soul
Balancing Body, Mind, and Spirit through Traditional Jewish Prayer, Movement, and
Meditation *By Tamar Frankiel, Ph.D., and Judy Greenfeld*
7 x 10, 184 pp, illus., Quality PB, ISBN 1-879045-64-8 **$16.95**
Audiotape of the Blessings and Meditations: 60 min. **$9.95**
Videotape of the Movements and Meditations: 46 min. **$20.00**

Spirituality/Women's Interest

Lifecycles, Vol. 1: Jewish Women on Life Passages & Personal Milestones
Edited and with introductions by Rabbi Debra Orenstein
6 x 9, 480 pp, Quality PB, ISBN 1-58023-018-0 **$19.95**

Lifecycles, Vol. 2: Jewish Women on Biblical Themes in Contemporary Life
Edited and with introductions by Rabbi Debra Orenstein and Rabbi Jane Rachel Litman
6 x 9, 464 pp, Quality PB, ISBN 1-58023-019-9 **$19.95**

Moonbeams: A Hadassah Rosh Hodesh Guide *Edited by Carol Diament, Ph.D.*
8½ x 11, 240 pp, Quality PB, ISBN 1-58023-099-7 **$20.00**

ReVisions: Seeing Torah through a Feminist Lens *By Rabbi Elyse Goldstein*
5½ x 8½, 224 pp, Quality PB, ISBN 1-58023-117-9 **$16.95**

White Fire: A Portrait of Women Spiritual Leaders in America
By Rabbi Malka Drucker. Photographs by Gay Block.
7 x 10, 320 pp, 30+ b/w photos, Hardcover, ISBN 1-893361-64-0 **$24.95** *(A SkyLight Paths book)*

Women of the Wall: Claiming Sacred Ground at Judaism's Holy Site
Edited by Phyllis Chesler and Rivka Haut
6 x 9, 496 pp, b/w photos, Hardcover, ISBN 1-58023-161-6 **$34.95**

The Women's Haftarah Commentary: New Insights from Women Rabbis on
the 54 Weekly Haftarah Portions, the 5 Megillot & Special Shabbatot
Edited by Rabbi Elyse Goldstein 6 x 9, 560 pp, Hardcover, ISBN 1-58023-133-0 **$39.99**

The Women's Torah Commentary: New Insights from Women Rabbis on the 54
Weekly Torah Portions *Edited by Rabbi Elyse Goldstein*
6 x 9, 496 pp, Hardcover, ISBN 1-58023-076-8 **$34.95**

The Year Mom Got Religion: One Woman's Midlife Journey into Judaism
By Lee Meyerhoff Hendler
6 x 9, 208 pp, Quality PB, ISBN 1-58023-070-9 **$15.95**; Hardcover, ISBN 1-58023-000-8 **$19.95**

See Holidays for *The Women's Passover Companion: Women's Reflections on
the Festival of Freedom* and *The Women's Seder Sourcebook: Rituals &
Readings for Use at the Passover Seder.*

Travel

Israel—A Spiritual Travel Guide: A Companion for the Modern Jewish Pilgrim
By Rabbi Lawrence A. Hoffman 4¾ x 10, 256 pp, Quality PB, illus., ISBN 1-879045-56-7 **$18.95**
Also Available: **The Israel Mission Leader's Guide** ISBN 1-58023-085-7 **$4.95**

12 Steps

100 Blessings Every Day
Daily Twelve Step Recovery Affirmations, Exercises for Personal Growth &
Renewal Reflecting Seasons of the Jewish Year
By Rabbi Kerry M. Olitzky. Foreword by Rabbi Neil Gillman.
Using a one-day-at-a-time monthly format, this guide reflects on the rhythm of
the Jewish calendar to help bring insight to recovery from addictions and com-
pulsive behaviors of all kinds. Its exercises help us move from *thinking* to *doing.*
4½ x 6½, 432 pp, Quality PB, ISBN 1-879045-30-3 **$14.99**

Recovery from Codependence: A Jewish Twelve Steps Guide to Healing Your Soul
By Rabbi Kerry M. Olitzky 6 x 9, 160 pp, Quality PB, ISBN 1-879045-32-X **$13.95**

Renewed Each Day: Daily Twelve Step Recovery Meditations Based on the Bible
By Rabbi Kerry M. Olitzky and Aaron Z.
Vol. 1—Genesis & Exodus:
6 x 9, 224 pp, Quality PB, ISBN 1-879045-12-5 **$14.95**
Vol. 2—Leviticus, Numbers & Deuteronomy:
6 x 9, 280 pp, Quality PB, ISBN 1-879045-13-3 **$14.95**

Twelve Jewish Steps to Recovery
A Personal Guide to Turning from Alcoholism & Other Addictions—Drugs, Food,
Gambling, Sex...
By Rabbi Kerry M. Olitzky and Stuart A. Copans, M.D. Preface by Abraham J. Twerski, M.D.
6 x 9, 144 pp, Quality PB, ISBN 1-879045-09-5 **$14.95**

Theology/Philosophy

Aspects of Rabbinic Theology
By Solomon Schechter. New Introduction by Dr. Neil Gillman.
6 x 9, 448 pp, Quality PB, ISBN 1-879045-24-9 **$19.95**

Broken Tablets: Restoring the Ten Commandments and Ourselves
Edited by Rachel S. Mikva. Introduction by Lawrence Kushner. Afterword by Arnold Jacob Wolf.
6 x 9, 192 pp, Quality PB, ISBN 1-58023-158-6 **$16.95**; Hardcover, ISBN 1-58023-066-0 **$21.95**

Creating an Ethical Jewish Life
A Practical Introduction to Classic Teachings on How to Be a Jew
By Dr. Byron L. Sherwin and Seymour J. Cohen
6 x 9, 336 pp, Quality PB, ISBN 1-58023-114-4 **$19.95**

The Death of Death: Resurrection and Immortality in Jewish Thought
By Dr. Neil Gillman 6 x 9, 336 pp, Quality PB, ISBN 1-58023-081-4 **$18.95**

Evolving Halakhah: A Progressive Approach to Traditional Jewish Law
By Rabbi Dr. Moshe Zemer
6 x 9, 480 pp, Quality PB, ISBN 1-58023-127-6 **$29.95**; Hardcover, ISBN 1-58023-002-4 **$40.00**

Hasidic Tales: Annotated & Explained
By Rabbi Rami Shapiro. Foreword by Andrew Harvey, SkyLight Illuminations series editor.
5½ x 8½, 240 pp, Quality PB, ISBN 1-893361-86-1 **$16.95** *(A SkyLight Paths Book)*

A Heart of Many Rooms: Celebrating the Many Voices within Judaism
By Dr. David Hartman
6 x 9, 352 pp, Quality PB, ISBN 1-58023-156-X **$19.95**; Hardcover, ISBN 1-58023-048-2 **$24.95**

Judaism and Modern Man: An Interpretation of Jewish Religion
By Will Herberg. New Introduction by Dr. Neil Gillman.
5½ x 8½, 336 pp, Quality PB, ISBN 1-879045-87-7 **$18.95**

Keeping Faith with the Psalms: Deepen Your Relationship with God Using the
Book of Psalms *By Daniel F. Polish*
6 x 9, 272 pp, Hardcover, ISBN 1-58023-179-9 **$24.95**

The Last Trial
On the Legends and Lore of the Command to Abraham to Offer Isaac as a Sacrifice
By Shalom Spiegel. New Introduction by Judah Goldin.
6 x 9, 208 pp, Quality PB, ISBN 1-879045-29-X **$18.95**

A Living Covenant: The Innovative Spirit in Traditional Judaism
By Dr. David Hartman 6 x 9, 368 pp, Quality PB, ISBN 1-58023-011-3 **$18.95**

Love and Terror in the God Encounter
The Theological Legacy of Rabbi Joseph B. Soloveitchik
By Dr. David Hartman
6 x 9, 240 pp, Quality PB, ISBN 1-58023-176-4 **$19.95**; Hardcover, ISBN 1-58023-112-8 **$25.00**

Seeking the Path to Life
Theological Meditations on God and the Nature of People, Love, Life and Death
By Rabbi Ira F. Stone 6 x 9, 160 pp, Quality PB, ISBN 1-879045-47-8 **$14.95**

The Spirit of Renewal: Finding Faith after the Holocaust
By Rabbi Edward Feld 6 x 9, 224 pp, Quality PB, ISBN 1-879045-40-0 **$16.95**

Tormented Master: *The Life and Spiritual Quest of Rabbi Nahman of Bratslav*
By Dr. Arthur Green 6 x 9, 416 pp, Quality PB, ISBN 1-879045-11-7 **$19.99**

Your Word Is Fire: The Hasidic Masters on Contemplative Prayer
Edited and translated by Dr. Arthur Green and Barry W. Holtz
6 x 9, 160 pp, Quality PB, ISBN 1-879045-25-7 **$15.95**

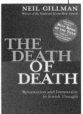

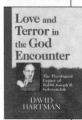

I Am Jewish
Personal Reflections Inspired by the Last Words of Daniel Pearl
Almost 150 Jews—both famous and not—from all walks of life, from all around
the world, write about Identity, Heritage, Covenant/Chosenness and Faith,
Humanity and Ethnicity, and *Tikkun Olam* and Justice.
Edited by Judea and Ruth Pearl
6 x 9, 304 pp, Hardcover, ISBN 1-58023-183-7 **$24.99**

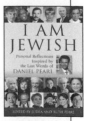

About Jewish Lights

People of all faiths and backgrounds yearn for books that attract, engage, educate, and spiritually inspire.

Our principal goal is to stimulate thought and help all people learn about who the Jewish People are, where they come from, and what the future can be made to hold. While people of our diverse Jewish heritage are the primary audience, our books speak to people in the Christian world as well and will broaden their understanding of Judaism and the roots of their own faith.

We bring to you authors who are at the forefront of spiritual thought and experience. While each has something different to say, they all say it in a voice that you can hear.

Our books are designed to welcome you and then to engage, stimulate, and inspire. We judge our success not only by whether or not our books are beautiful and commercially successful, but by whether or not they make a difference in your life.

For your information and convenience, at the back of this book we have provided a list of other Jewish Lights books you might find interesting and useful. They cover all the categories of your life:

Bar/Bat Mitzvah	Life Cycle
Bible Study / Midrash	Meditation
Children's Books	Parenting
Congregation Resources	Prayer
Current Events / History	Ritual / Sacred Practice
Ecology	Spirituality
Fiction: Mystery, Science Fiction	Theology / Philosophy
Grief / Healing	Travel
Holidays / Holy Days	Twelve Steps
Inspiration	Women's Interest
Kabbalah / Mysticism / Enneagram	

Stuart M. Matlins, Publisher

Or phone, fax, mail or e-mail to: **JEWISH LIGHTS Publishing**
Sunset Farm Offices, Route 4 • P.O. Box 237 • Woodstock, Vermont 05091
Tel: (802) 457-4000 • Fax: (802) 457-4004 • www.jewishlights.com
Credit card orders: (800) 962-4544 (8:30AM–5:30PM ET Monday–Friday)
Generous discounts on quantity orders. SATISFACTION GUARANTEED. Prices subject to change.

For more information about each book, visit our website at www.jewishlights.com